W9-AYU-133

Teach Yourself
VISUALLY™
Dreamweaver® CS3

Visual™

by Janine C. Warner

S

BICENTENNIAL
1807
WILEY
2007
BICENTENNIAL

Wiley Publishing, Inc.

Teach Yourself VISUALLY™ Dreamweaver® CS3

Published by
Wiley Publishing, Inc.
111 River Street
Hoboken, NJ 07030-5774

Published simultaneously in Canada

Copyright © 2007 by Wiley Publishing, Inc., Indianapolis, Indiana

No part of this publication may be reproduced, stored in a retrieval system or transmitted in any form or by any means, electronic, mechanical, photocopying, recording, scanning or otherwise, except as permitted under Sections 107 or 108 of the 1976 United States Copyright Act, without either the prior written permission of the Publisher, or authorization through payment of the appropriate per-copy fee to the Copyright Clearance Center, 222 Rosewood Drive, Danvers, MA 01923, (978) 750-8400, fax (978) 646-8600. Requests to the Publisher for permission should be addressed to the Legal Department, Wiley Publishing, Inc., 10475 Crosspoint Blvd., Indianapolis, IN 46256, (317) 572-3447, fax (317) 572-4355, Online: www.wiley.com/go/permissions.

Library of Congress Control Number: 2007926014

ISBN: 978-0-470-14475-6

Manufactured in the United States of America

10 9 8 7 6 5 4 3 2 1

Trademark Acknowledgments

Contact Us

For general information on our other products and services please contact our Customer Care Department within the U.S. at 800-762-2974, outside the U.S. at 317-572-3993 or fax 317-572-4002.

For technical support please visit www.wiley.com/techsupport.

Wiley Publishing, Inc.

Sales

Contact Wiley at (800) 762-2974 or fax (317) 572-4002.

Praise for Visual Books

"Like a lot of other people, I understand things best when I see them visually. Your books really make learning easy and life more fun."

John T. Frey (Cadillac, MI)

"I have quite a few of your Visual books and have been very pleased with all of them. I love the way the lessons are presented!"

Mary Jane Newman (Yorba Linda, CA)

"I just purchased my third Visual book (my first two are dog-eared now!), and, once again, your product has surpassed my expectations.

Tracey Moore (Memphis, TN)

"I am an avid fan of your Visual books. If I need to learn anything, I just buy one of your books and learn the topic in no time. Wonders! I have even trained my friends to give me Visual books as gifts."

Illona Bergstrom (Aventura, FL)

"Thank you for making it so clear. I appreciate it. I will buy many more Visual books."

J.P. Sangdong (North York, Ontario, Canada)

"I have several books from the Visual series and have always found them to be valuable resources."

Stephen P. Miller (Ballston Spa, NY)

"Thank you for the wonderful books you produce. It wasn't until I was an adult that I discovered how I learn – visually. Nothing compares to Visual books. I love the simple layout. I can just grab a book and use it at my computer, lesson by lesson. And I understand the material! You really know the way I think and learn. Thanks so much!"

Stacey Han (Avondale, AZ)

"I absolutely admire your company's work. Your books are terrific. The format is perfect, especially for visual learners like me. Keep them coming!"

Frederick A. Taylor, Jr. (New Port Richey, FL)

"I have several of your Visual books and they are the best I have ever used."

Stanley Clark (Crawfordville, FL)

"I bought my first Teach Yourself VISUALLY book last month. Wow. Now I want to learn everything in this easy format!"

Tom Vial (New York, NY)

"Thank you, thank you, thank you...for making it so easy for me to break into this high-tech world. I now own four of your books. I recommend them to anyone who is a beginner like myself."

Gay O'Donnell (Calgary, Alberta, Canada)

"I write to extend my thanks and appreciation for your books. They are clear, easy to follow, and straight to the point. Keep up the good work! I bought several of your books and they are just right! No regrets! I will always buy your books because they are the best."

Seward Kollie (Dakar, Senegal)

"Compliments to the chef!! Your books are extraordinary! Or, simply put, extra-ordinary, meaning way above the rest! THANK YOU THANK YOU THANK YOU! I buy them for friends, family, and colleagues."

Christine J. Manfrin (Castle Rock, CO)

"What fantastic teaching books you have produced! Congratulations to you and your staff. You deserve the Nobel Prize in Education in the Software category. Thanks for helping me understand computers."

Bruno Tonon (Melbourne, Australia)

"Over time, I have bought a number of your 'Read Less - Learn More' books. For me, they are THE way to learn anything easily. I learn easiest using your method of teaching."

José A. Mazón (Cuba, NY)

"I am an avid purchaser and reader of the Visual series, and they are the greatest computer books I've seen. The Visual books are perfect for people like myself who enjoy the computer, but want to know how to use it more efficiently. Your books have definitely given me a greater understanding of my computer, and have taught me to use it more effectively. Thank you very much for the hard work, effort, and dedication that you put into this series."

Alex Diaz (Las Vegas, NV)

Credits

Project Editor
Tim Borek

Acquisitions Editor
Jody Lefevere

Copy Editor
Marylouise Wiack

Technical Editor
David LaFontaine

Editorial Manager
Robyn Siesky

Business Manager
Amy Knies

Manufacturing
Allan Conley
Linda Cook
Paul Gilchrist
Jennifer Guynn

Book Design
Kathie Rickard

Production Coordinator
Adrienne Martinez

Layout
Carrie A. Foster
Jennifer Mayberry
Melanee Prendergast
Heather Ryan
Amanda Spagnuolo

Screen Artist
Jill Proll

Illustrators
Ronda David-Burroughs
Cheryl Grubbs

Graphics
Joyce Haughey

Proofreader
Laura Bowman

Quality Control
Dwight Ramsey

Indexer
Infodex Indexing
Services Inc.

Special Help
Alissa Birkel
Jade Williams

**Vice President and Executive
Group Publisher**
Richard Swadley

Vice President and Publisher
Barry Pruett

Composition Director
Debbie Stailey

Wiley Bicentennial Logo
Richard J. Pacifico

About the Author

Janine Warner's expertise in media, technology, and cross-cultural business has taken her on consulting assignments from Miami to Mexico and speaking engagements from New York to New Delhi.

Since 1996, she has authored more than a dozen books about the Internet, including *Creating Family Web Sites For Dummies* and the best-selling *Dreamweaver For Dummies* (now in its sixth edition).

Her success as an author attracted the attention of Total Training, Inc., a pioneer in innovative video-based training, where she was first contracted in 2005 to host a video called *Total Training for Dreamweaver CS2.* Her first video won two industry awards and she is now working on a series of Web design videos that includes Advanced Dreamweaver CS3.

An award-winning journalist, her articles and columns have appeared in a variety of publications, including *The Miami Herald, Shape Magazine,* and the Pulitzer Prize-winning *Point Reyes Light* newspaper. She also writes a regular column on Dreamweaver for *Layers Magazine.*

Janine has taught online journalism at the University of Southern California Annenberg School for Communication and the University of Miami. In 1998, she joined *The Miami Herald* as Online Managing Editor. A year later, she was promoted to Director of New Media. She left that position to serve as Director of Latin American Operations for CNET Networks, an international technology media company.

Since 2001, Warner has run her own business as a writer, speaker, and consultant. She earned a degree in journalism and Spanish from the University of Massachusetts, Amherst, and spent the first several years of her career in Northern California as a reporter and editor. She lives with her husband in Los Angeles.

Author's Acknowledgments

This book is dedicated to everyone who wants to share ideas, stories, and business ventures over the Internet. I wish you all the best and thank you for supporting my books and videos. I love teaching Web design because it's so much fun to see what everyone creates.

Special thanks to Frank Vera, a great programmer who helped with the most technical chapter of the book, Chapter 16. Thanks also to the many Web designers whose work is featured in this book, including Sheila Castelli and Davi Cheng.

Thanks to my entire family, most notably my adorable nieces, Mikayla, Savannah, and Jessica, whose photos appear in some of the screen shots in the book.

And finally, thanks to the entire team at Wiley Publishing, especially Tim Borek and Jody Lefevere.

Table of Contents

chapter 1   Getting Started with Dreamweaver

chapter 2   Setting Up Your Web Site

chapter **3** Exploring the Dreamweaver Interface

chapter **4** Working with HTML

Table of Contents

chapter 5   Formatting and Styling Text

chapter 6   Working with Images and Multimedia

chapter 7 Creating Hyperlinks

chapter 8 Editing Table Designs in a Web Page

Table of Contents

chapter 11   Using Library Items and Templates

chapter 12   Creating and Applying Cascading Style Sheets

Table of Contents

chapter 13 — Designing a Web Site with CSS

chapter 14 — Publishing a Web Site

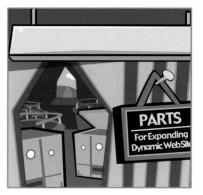

How to Use This Book

How to Use This Teach Yourself VISUALLY Book

Do you look at the pictures in a book or newspaper before anything else on a page? Would you rather see an image instead of read about how to do something? Search no further. This book is for you. Opening *Teach Yourself VISUALLY Dreamweaver CS3* allows you to read less and learn more about the Dreamweaver program.

Who Needs This Book

This book is for a reader who has never used this particular technology or software application. It is also for more computer literate individuals who want to expand their knowledge of the different features that Dreamweaver has to offer. We assume you already have basic computer experience, but want to learn the specifics of building Web sites with Dreamweaver.

Book Organization

Teach Yourself VISUALLY Dreamweaver CS3 has 16 chapters.

Chapter Organization

This book consists of sections, all listed in the book's table of contents. A *section* is a set of steps that show you how to complete a specific computer task.

Each section, usually contained on two facing pages, has an introduction to the task at hand, a set of full-color screen shots and steps that walk you through the task, and a set of tips. This format allows you to quickly look at a topic of interest and learn it instantly.

Chapters group together three or more sections with a common theme. A chapter may also contain pages that give you the background information needed to understand the sections in a chapter.

What You Need to Use This Book

Using the Mouse

This book uses the following conventions to describe the actions you perform when using the mouse:

Click

Press your left mouse button once. You generally click your mouse on something to select something on the screen.

Double-click

Press your left mouse button twice. Double-clicking something on the computer screen generally opens whatever item you have double-clicked.

Right-click

Press your right mouse button. When you right-click anything on the computer screen, the program displays a shortcut menu containing commands specific to the selected item.

Click and Drag, and Release the Mouse

Move your mouse pointer and hover it over an item on the screen. Press and hold down the left mouse button. Now, move the mouse to where you want to place the item and then release the button. You use this method to move an item from one area of the computer screen to another.

The Conventions in This Book

A number of typographic and layout styles have been used throughout *Teach Yourself VISUALLY Dreamweaver CS3* to distinguish different types of information.

Bold

Bold type represents the names of commands and options that you interact with. Bold type also indicates text and numbers that you must type into a dialog box or window.

Italics

Italic words introduce a new term and are followed by a definition.

Numbered Steps

You must perform the instructions in numbered steps in order to successfully complete a section and achieve the final results.

Bulleted Steps

These steps point out various optional features. You do not have to perform these steps; they simply give additional information about a feature.

Indented Text

Indented text tells you what the program does in response to you following a numbered step. For example, if you click a certain menu command, a dialog box may appear, or a window may open. Indented text may also tell you what the final result is when you follow a set of numbered steps.

Notes

Notes give additional information. They may describe special conditions that may occur during an operation. They may warn you of a situation that you want to avoid, for example the loss of data. A note may also cross-reference a related area of the book. A cross-reference may guide you to another chapter, or another section within the current chapter.

Icons and Buttons

Icons and buttons are graphical representations within the text. They show you exactly what you need to click to perform a step.

 You can easily identify the tips in any section by looking for the TIPS icon. Tips offer additional information, including tips, hints, and tricks. You can use the TIPS information to go beyond what you have learned in the steps.

Getting Started with Dreamweaver

This chapter describes the World Wide Web, introduces the different types of information that you can put on a Web site, and shows you how to start Dreamweaver.

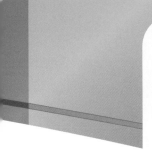

Introduction to the World Wide Web

You can use Dreamweaver to create and publish pages on the World Wide Web.

World Wide Web

The World Wide Web—or simply the Web—is a global collection of documents located on Internet-connected computers. You can access the Web by using a Web browser. Web pages are connected to one another by hyperlinks that you can click.

Web Site

A Web site is a collection of linked Web pages stored on a Web server. Most Web sites have a home page that describes the information located on the Web site and provides a place where people can start their exploration of the Web site. The pages of a good Web site are intuitively organized and have a common theme.

Dreamweaver

Dreamweaver is a program that enables you to create Web pages with hyperlinks, text, images, and multimedia. You can create your Web pages on your computer and then use Dreamweaver to transfer the finished files to a Web server where others can view them on the Web.

HTML

Hypertext Markup Language (HTML) is the formatting language that is used to create Web pages. You can use Dreamweaver to create Web pages without knowing HTML because Dreamweaver writes the HTML for you behind the scenes.

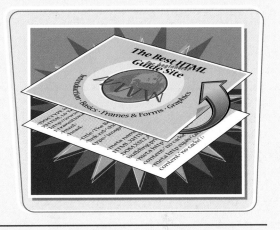

Web Server

A Web server is a computer that is connected to the Internet and has software that serves Web pages to visitors. Each Web page that you view in a Web browser on the World Wide Web resides on a Web server somewhere on the Internet. When you are ready to publish your pages on the Web, you can use Dreamweaver to transfer your files to a Web server.

Web Browser

A Web browser is a program that can download Web documents from the Internet, interpret HTML, and then display the Web page text and any associated images and multimedia. Two popular Web browsers are Microsoft Internet Explorer and Netscape Navigator.

The Many Ways to Design a Web Page

In the early days of the Internet, Web design was easy but boring. Today, there are many more ways to design Web pages, but first you have to decide which approach is best for your site. Here are a few of the options that you can choose.

Text and Images

Inserting text and images into a Web page is the simplest design option. Dreamweaver makes it easy to add images and text and to change the size, color, and font of the text on your Web page. It also makes it easy to organize text into paragraphs, headings, and lists, and to change alignment. However, if you want to create a more complex design, you need to use one of the other options described in this section.

Tables

Tables have long been a popular choice for creating page designs. By merging and splitting table cells, you can create complex layouts using tables. By turning off the border, you can make the actual table invisible. Tables are quickly being replaced by CSS layouts. However, they are still recommended for tabular data (such as the kind of information you would find in a spreadsheet program). There are also still many Web sites that use tables to position images, text, and other elements on a page.

Frames

In a framed Web site, the Web browser window is divided into several rectangular frames, and a different Web page loads into each frame. Users can scroll through content in each frame, independent of the content in the other frames. Dreamweaver offers visual tools for building frame-based Web sites. Many designers recommend against using frames because they create pages that are hard to bookmark, they do not work as well in search engines, and navigating around frames can be confusing to visitors.

AP Divs

Dreamweaver's AP Divs (called *layers* in Dreamweaver CS3) use absolute positioning to create "boxes" that you can use to position images, text, and other content on a page. AP Divs are very intuitive to use: You just click and drag to create a box anywhere on a Web page. Their biggest limitation is that they can only be aligned to the left side of the page; as a result, you cannot center designs with this technique. Another limitation is that, although they seem to give you precise design control, their display can vary dramatically from browser to browser.

CSS Layouts

Many professional Web designers today recommend creating page layouts using Cascading Style Sheets (CSS). Although AP Divs (described in the previous section) are technically CSS layouts, they receive very special treatment in Dreamweaver and have some very significant limitations. When designers refer to CSS layouts, they generally mean designs that do not use absolute positioning (or that use it very sparingly). Using CSS is one of the most challenging Web design options, but it brings some powerful benefits, such as greater accessibility and flexibility, which can help your site look better to more people on a greater range of devices. When used effectively, pages designed with CSS are also faster to download and easier to update.

Adobe Flash

Some of the "flashiest" sites on the Web have been created using Adobe Flash, a vector-based design program that you can use to create animations and highly advanced interactive features. Although you can use Dreamweaver to add Flash files to your Web pages and to create some basic Flash elements, such as Flash buttons, you should know that many of the most elaborate multimedia sites on the Web were created using Flash, and not just Dreamweaver.

Dynamic Web Sites

At the highest end of the Web design spectrum, you can connect a Web site to a database to create highly interactive sites with features such as shopping carts, discussion boards, and more. Database-driven sites are especially useful when a Web site grows to more than 100 pages or so, because they are much more efficient to update. You can learn more about Dreamweaver's database features in the final chapter of this book.

Plan Your Web Site

Carefully planning your pages before you build them can help to ensure that your finished Web site looks great and is well organized. Before you start building your Web site, take a little time to organize your ideas and gather the materials that you will need.

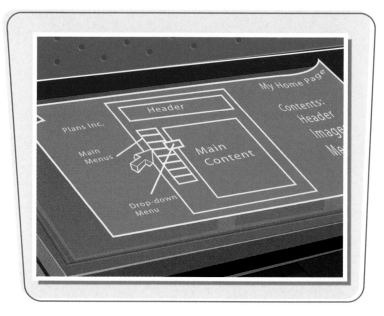

Organize Your Ideas

Build your Web site on paper before you start building it in Dreamweaver. Sketching out a Web site map, with rectangles representing Web pages and arrows representing links, can help you to visualize the size and scope of your project. Use sticky notes if you want to move pages around as you plan your Web site.

Gather Your Content

Before you start building your Web site, gather all of the elements that you want to use. This process may require writing text, taking photos, and designing graphics. It can also involve producing multimedia content, such as audio and video files. Gathering all of your material together in the beginning makes it easier for you to organize your Web site once you start building it in Dreamweaver.

Define Your Audience

Identifying your target audience can help you to decide what kind of content to offer on your Web site. For example, you may create a very different design for small children than for adults. It is important to know whether visitors are using the latest Web browser technology and how fast they can view advanced features, such as multimedia.

Host Your Finished Web Site

To make your finished Web site accessible on the Web, you need to store, or host, it on a Web server. Most people have their Web sites hosted on a Web server at a commercial Internet service provider (ISP) or at their company or university.

Start Dreamweaver on a PC

You can start Dreamweaver on a PC and begin building pages that you can publish on the Web. You first need to purchase and install Dreamweaver if you do not have it already. You can also download a free, trial version at www.adobe.com.

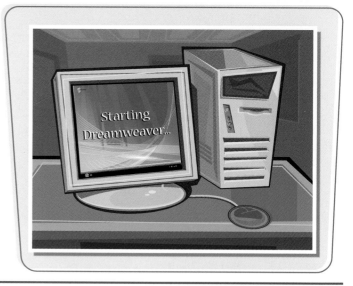

Start Dreamweaver on a PC

① Click **Start**.

② Click **All Programs**.

③ Click **Adobe Web Premium CS3**.

④ Click **Adobe Dreamweaver CS3**.

Note: Your path to the Dreamweaver application may be different, depending on how you installed your software and your operating system.

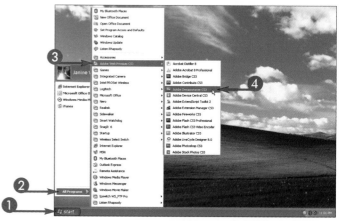

● The Dreamweaver start screen appears.

Start Dreamweaver on a Macintosh

You can start Dreamweaver on a Macintosh and begin building pages that you can publish on the Web. You first need to purchase and install Dreamweaver if you do not have it already. You can also download a free, trial version at www.adobe.com.

Start Dreamweaver on a Macintosh

① Double-click your hard drive icon.

② Click here to open the **Adobe Dreamweaver CS3** folder (Dw).

③ Double-click the **Dreamweaver CS3** icon (Dw).

Note: *The exact location of the Dreamweaver folder depends on how you installed your software.*

● The Dreamweaver Welcome Screen appears.

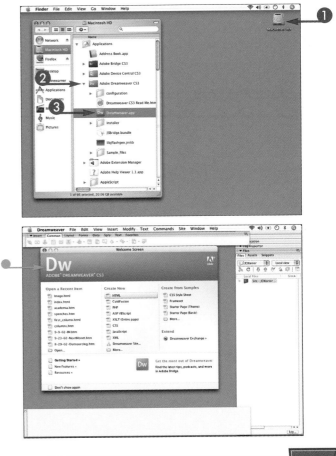

Dreamweaver CS3 on a PC features a variety of windows, panels, and inspectors.

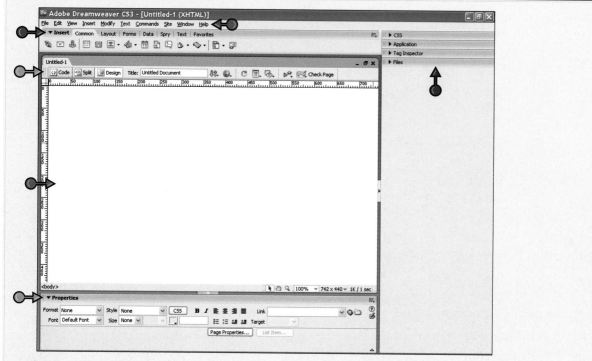

Toolbar

Contains shortcuts to preview and display features, and a test field where you can specify the title of a page.

Menus

Contains the commands for using Dreamweaver. Many of these commands are duplicated within the windows, panels, and inspectors of Dreamweaver.

Insert Bar

Provides easy access to common features. There are several different insert bars that you can select, depending on the type of features you want to insert in your page.

Property Inspector

Used to display and edit attributes of any element selected in the Document window.

Panels

Windows that provide access to the Design, Code, Application, Tag, Files, Layers, and History panels.

Document Window

The main workspace where you insert and arrange the text, images, and other elements of your Web page.

Dreamweaver CS3 on a Macintosh features a variety of windows, panels, and inspectors.

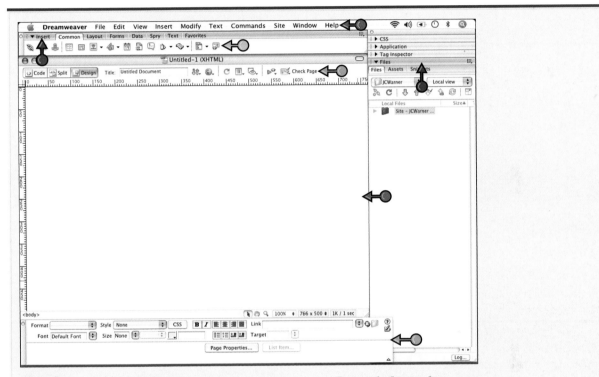

Toolbar

Contains shortcuts to preview and display features, and a test field where you can specify the title of a page.

Menus

Contains the commands for using Dreamweaver. Many of these commands are duplicated within the windows, panels, and inspectors of Dreamweaver.

Insert Bar

Provides easy access to common features. There are several different insert bars that you can select, depending on the type of features you want to insert in your page.

Property Inspector

Used to display and edit attributes of any element selected in the Document window.

Panels

Windows that provide access to the Design, Code, Application, Tag, Files, Layers, and History panels.

Document Window

The main workspace where you insert and arrange the text, images, and other elements of your Web page.

You can show or hide accessory windows, also called panels and inspectors, by using commands in the Window menu.

Show or Hide a Window

① Click **Window**.

② Click the name of the window, panel, or inspector that you want to open.

This example opens the Property inspector.

● A check mark next to a name indicates that the window, panel, or inspector is open.

● Dreamweaver displays the inspector.

To hide a window, panel, or inspector, you can click **Window** and then click the check-marked (✓) name.

You can click **Window** and then click **Hide Panels** to hide everything except the Document window and toolbar.

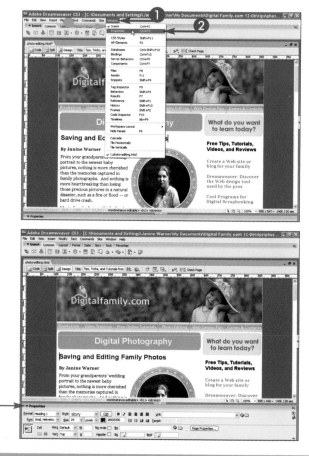

You can exit Dreamweaver to close the program.

You should always exit Dreamweaver and all other programs before turning off your computer.

Exit Dreamweaver

① Click **File**.

② Click **Exit**.

Before quitting, Dreamweaver alerts you to save any open documents that have unsaved changes.

③ Click **Yes**.

Dreamweaver exits.

Get Help

You can use the help tools that are built into Dreamweaver to find answers to your questions or to learn techniques that you do not know.

① Click **Help**.

② Click **Dreamweaver Help**.

● You can also click the **Help** icon (⦾) in the Property inspector.

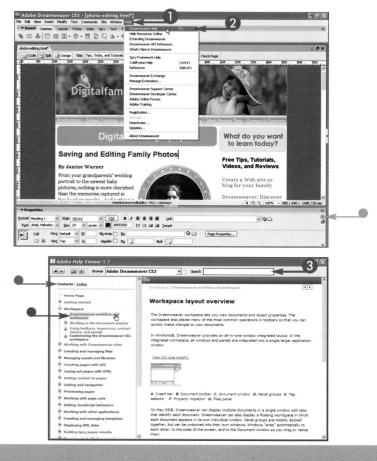

The Using Dreamweaver help page opens.

● You can click the **Contents** tab to view available help topics.

● You can click any topic to display the results in the help window.

③ You can search for a topic in Dreamweaver Help by typing one or more keywords into the Search field.

④ Press Enter (Return).

A list of topics appears.

● You can narrow your search by entering keywords separated by a plus sign.

⑤ Click a topic from the search result list.

Information appears on the topic you selected.

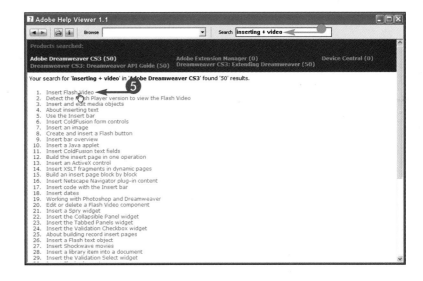

Are there different ways of opening the help tools and other options in Dreamweaver?

Very often, yes. As with many programs, there is often more than one way to do the same task. For example, you can access many tools and commands, such as Modify Page Properties, by using either a menu or the Property inspector. You can also use the Split or Code view commands to view and edit the HTML code directly, if you know how to write HTML.

CHAPTER 2

Setting Up Your Web Site

You start a project in Dreamweaver by defining a local root folder where you will store all of the files in your Web site on your computer. You can then create your first page and save it in the root folder. This chapter shows you how to set up your Web site.

Define a New Web Site

Before you create your Web pages, you need to define your site in Dreamweaver and set up a root folder where you can store all of the files in your site. Defining a root site folder enables Dreamweaver to manage your files in the Files panel and properly set links. As you set up your site, you can create a new folder on your hard drive or select an existing folder as your root folder. For more information on the Files panel, see Chapter 14.

Define a New Web Site

① Click the **Manage Sites** link.

The Manage Sites dialog box appears.

② Click **New**.

③ Click **Site**.

The Site Definition dialog box appears.

④ Click the **Advanced** tab.

⑤ Type a name for your site.

⑥ Click the folder icon (📁) to search for your Web site folder.

The Choose Local Root Folder dialog box appears.

⑦ Click here and select the folder that stores your Web pages.

● You can create a new folder by clicking 📄, typing in a new name for the folder, and then selecting the new folder.

⑧ Click **Select**.

⑨ Click 📁 and select the folder where you want to store the images for your Web site.

⑩ Type the URL (Web address or domain name) of your Web site.

⑪ Click this option to enable the cache, which makes it faster to create links (☐ changes to ✓).

⑫ Click **OK**.

⑬ In the Manage Sites window, click **Done**.

TIP

Why is it important to keep all of my Web site files in the same root folder on my computer?

Keeping everything in the same root folder on your local computer enables you to easily transfer your Web site files to a Web server without changing the organization of the files. If your Web site files are not organized on the Web server in the same way that they are organized on your local computer, then hyperlinks may not work, and images may not display properly. For more information about working with Web site files, see Chapter 14.

When you launch Dreamweaver CS3, the initial Start page opens. There are many useful shortcuts on this page, including some for creating a new Web page.

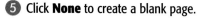

① Click **File**.

② Click **New**.

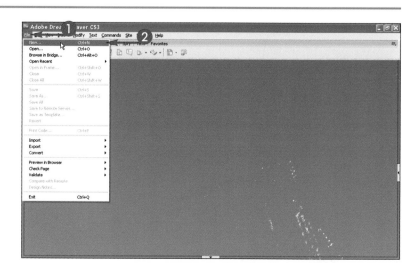

The New Document dialog box appears.

③ Click **Blank Page**.

④ Click **HTML** to specify the type of page.

⑤ Click **None** to create a blank page.

You can also create preformatted pages by choosing any of the other options under Layout in the New Document dialog box.

⑥ Click **Create**.

Dreamweaver displays a new Document window.

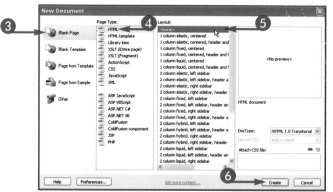

Add a Title to a Web Page

A Web page title appears in the title bar when the page opens in a Web browser. The title helps search engines to index pages with more accuracy, and is saved in a user's Bookmark list if they bookmark your Web page.

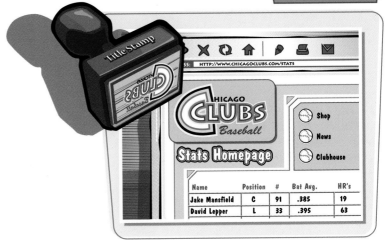

Add a Title to a Web Page

When you create a new document, an untitled document appears in the main workspace.

Note: *The page name and filename are "Untitled" until you save them.*

① Type a name for your Web page in the Title text box.

② Press Enter (Return).

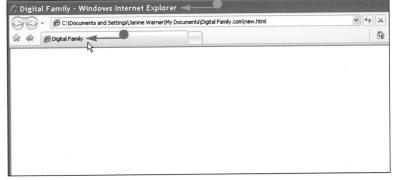

● The Web page title appears in the title bar when the page displays in a Web browser.

● If the browser supports tabbed browsing, the title also appears in the tab.

Save a
Web Page

You should save your Web page as soon as you create it, and again before closing the program or transferring the page to a remote site. It is also a good idea to save all of your files frequently to prevent work from being lost due to power outages or system failures. For more information about connecting to remote sites, see Chapter 14.

Save a Web Page

SAVE YOUR DOCUMENT

1 Click **File**.

2 Click **Save**.

● You can click **Save As** to save an existing file with a new filename.

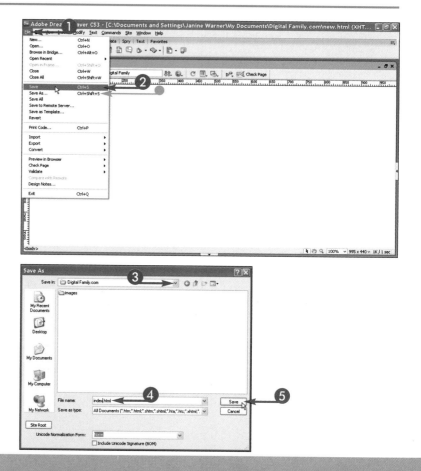

If you are saving a new file for the first time, the Save As dialog box appears.

3 Click here and select your local site folder.

Your local site folder is where you want to save the pages and other files for your Web site.

4 Type a name for your Web page.

5 Click **Save**.

● Dreamweaver saves the Web page, and the filename and path appear in the title bar.

● You can click ✖ to close the page.

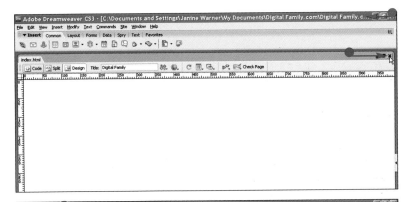

REVERT A PAGE

1 Click **File**.

2 Click **Revert**.

The page reverts to the previously saved version. All of the changes that you made since the last time you saved the file are lost.

Note: If you exit Dreamweaver after you save a document, Dreamweaver cannot revert to the previous version.

TIP

Why should I name the main page of my site index.html?
You should name your main Web site or home page index.html because that is the filename that most Web servers open first when a user types a domain name into a Web browser. If you name your main page index.html and it does not open as your first page when your site is on the server, then check with your system administrator or hosting service. Some servers use default.htm instead of index.html.

Preview a Web Page in a Browser

You can see how your Web page will appear online by previewing it in a Web browser. The Preview in Browser command works with any Web browser that is installed on your computer. Although Dreamweaver does not ship with Web browser software, Internet Explorer is preinstalled on most computers.

Preview a Web Page in a Browser

LAUNCH A WEB BROWSER

1. Click the **Preview in Browser** button (🖼).

2. Click a Web browser from the drop-down menu that appears.

   You can also preview the page in your primary Web browser by pressing F12.

   Your Web browser launches and opens the current page.

   When you preview a Web page in a browser, you can follow links by clicking them, just as you would when viewing Web sites.

ADD OR REMOVE A BROWSER

1 Click **File**.

2 Click **Preview in Browser**.

3 Click **Edit Browser List**.

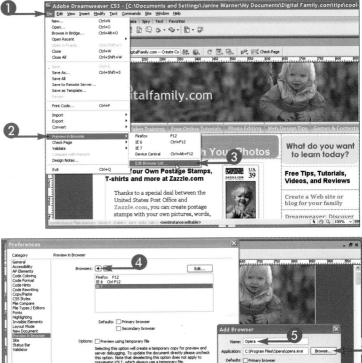

The Preferences dialog box appears.

4 Click the plus sign (➕).

The Add Browser dialog box appears.

5 Type a name for your Web browser.

6 Click **Browse** and select a Web browser for your computer.

7 Click **OK** to close the Add Browser dialog box.

8 Click **OK** to close the Preferences dialog box.

The newly added Web browser appears in the browser list.

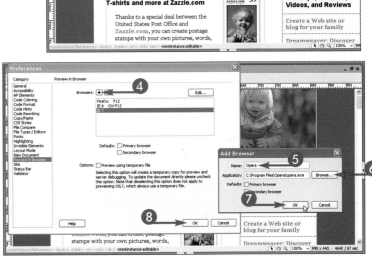

TIP

Why should I use more than one Web browser for previews?

Dreamweaver makes it easy for you to add more than one Web browser because not all Web browsers display Web pages the same way. For example, Internet Explorer and Firefox sometimes display Web pages differently. As a result, it is important to test your pages in a variety of browsers to ensure that they will look good to all of your visitors. By using the browser list, you can easily test your Web page in a different Web browser with just a few mouse-clicks, and adjust your designs until they look good in all of the browsers that you think your visitors may use.

Exploring the Dreamweaver Interface

Take a tour of the panels and windows that make up the Dreamweaver interface. You will discover all of the handy tools and features that make this an award-winning Web design program.

Customize the Document Window

The Document window is the main workspace in Dreamweaver, where you create Web pages and enter and format text, images, and other elements. You can open and close the customizable panels to keep the workspace clear when you are not using them.

Customize the Document Window

- You can click a tab to change the options in the Insert bar.

- The status bar displays the file size and estimated download time for the page.

① Click the ⫼ panels to open them.

The panels open.

- You can click ⫼ again to close the panels.

② Click the arrow (▽) in the Property inspector.

● The Property inspector expands to reveal additional options for any selected image or element.

③ Click **Split** (⊞ Split).

The Document window splits to display both the Code and Design views.

● When you select an element in one view, it is highlighted in the other view, thus making it easy to find formatting tags.

● You can hide the Code view by clicking **Design** (⊟ Design).

● You can click **Code** (⊡ Code) to view just the HTML code.

TIP

How can I keep my favorite features handy?

You can open or close any of the panels and inspectors in Dreamweaver so that your favorite features are handy when you need them, and so that others are out of the way when you do not need them. Most of the panels and other options are available from the Windows menu. For example, to open the History panel, you would click Window and then click History. As you work, you may choose to have different panels opened or closed to give you more workspace or to provide easier access to the features that you are using.

Format Content with the Property Inspector

The Property inspector enables you to view the properties associated with the object or text that is currently selected in the Document window. Text fields, drop-down menus, buttons, and other form elements in the Property inspector allow you to modify these properties.

Format Content with the Property Inspector

FORMAT AN IMAGE

① Click to select an image.

● The image properties appear.

You can change many image properties in the Property inspector, such as dimensions, filename, and alignment.

② To wrap the text around the image, click here and select an alignment.

● The text automatically wraps around the image when you apply Left alignment.

③ Click and drag to select text.

● The text properties appear.

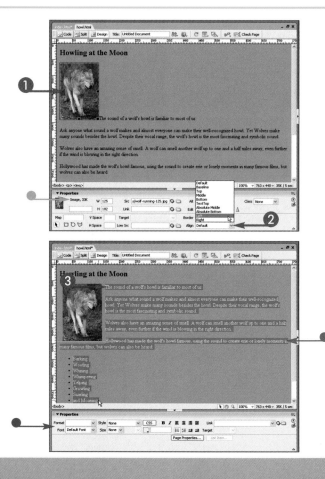

FORMAT TEXT

④ With the text selected, click the **Font** ▾.

⑤ Click the **Arial, Helvetica, sans-serif** font group.

These fonts are easy to read on a computer screen and are installed on most computers, so the page will display for the user as it does for the designer.

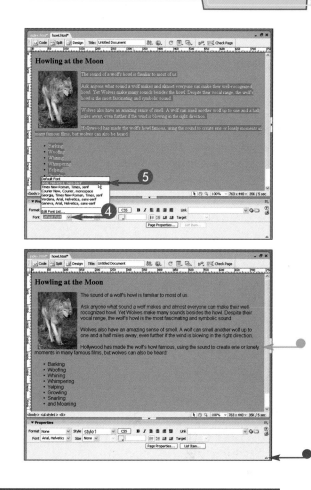

● Your text automatically changes to reflect your formatting choices in the Property inspector.

You can change many text properties in the Property inspector, such as format, size, and alignment.

● You can click ▾ to switch between standard and expanded modes for the Property inspector.

TIP

When would I use more than one font on a Web page?
When you choose a font face in Dreamweaver, the program offers fonts in groups of three. For example, one option is Arial, Helvetica, and sans-serif, and another option is Times New Roman, Times, and serif. Dreamweaver provides these collections because the fonts that display on a Web page are determined by the available fonts on the visitor's computer. Because you cannot guarantee what fonts a user will have, Web browsers use the first font that matches in a list of fonts. Thus, in the first example, the font will display as follows: in Arial if the Arial font is on the visitor's computer; in Helvetica if Arial is not available; in any available sans-serif font if neither of the first two fonts is available.

Add an E-Mail Link from the Insert Panel

You can insert elements, such as images, tables, and layers, into your pages with the Insert panel. Located at the top of the window, the panel features a drop-down menu that reveals options such as Common elements, Forms, and Text.

① Click the **Common tab**.

② Click and drag to select text.

③ Click the **Email Link** button (🖃).

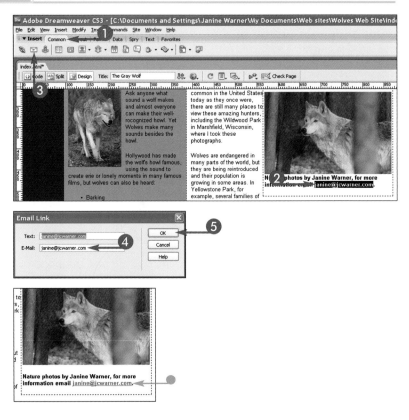

The Email Link dialog box appears.

④ Type an e-mail address.

⑤ Click **OK**.

● In this example, the text changes into an e-mail hyperlink.

You can click any button in the Insert panel to add that element to your document.

Correct Errors with the History Panel

The History panel keeps track of the commands that you perform in Dreamweaver. When you backtrack through those commands, you can return your page to a previous state. This is a convenient way to correct errors.

Correct Errors with the History Panel

1 Click **Window**.

2 Click **History**.

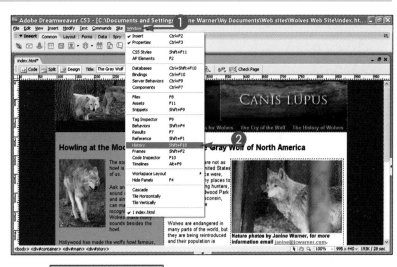

● The History panel appears.

● To undo one or more commands, you can click and drag the slider (🖿) upward.

To redo the commands, you can click and drag 🖿 downward.

Note: *If you move backward, the later changes are deleted. You can only add steps to the end of the sequence.*

Dreamweaver features an uncluttered workspace with windows that lock into place and panels that you can expand or collapse. You can also rearrange panels and move them around the screen to customize the interface.

1 Click **Window**.

2 Click **Files**.

● The Files panel appears and displays all of the files in the Web site.

3 Click the **Assets** tab.

The Assets panel appears.

4 Click the **Images** button ().

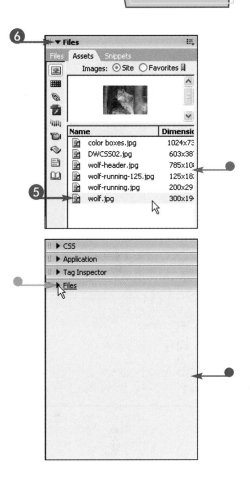

● All of the available images in the site appear in the Assets panel.

⑤ Click any image filename to preview the image in the display area at the top of the Assets panel.

⑥ Click the Files panel ▼ to close the Files panel.

● The Files and Assets panels collapse.

Note: *When you collapse a panel, such as the Files panel, other panels become more visible.*

● You can click ▶ to expand any panel.

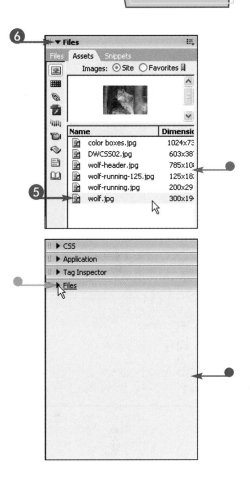

TIP

How can I keep track of my assets?
The Assets panel provides access to many handy features, such as the Colors assets, which list all of the colors that are used on a site. For example, this is useful if you are using a particular text color and you want to use the same color consistently on every page. Similarly, the Links assets make it easy to access links that are used elsewhere in your site so that you can quickly and easily set frequently used links.

Create and Apply a Custom Command

You can select a sequence of commands that have been recorded in the History panel, and save the sequence as a custom command. The new command appears under the Commands menu. You can then apply it to other elements on the page to automate repetitive tasks.

Create and Apply a Custom Command

SAVE A COMMAND SEQUENCE

① Select an element and perform a sequence of commands.

In this example, text is formatted in bold and italics.

If the History panel is not open, you can click **Window** and then click **History**.

② To select the steps that you want to save as a single command, Ctrl+click (⌘+click) each selection.

③ Right-click the selection.

④ Click **Save As Command**.

The Save As Command dialog box appears.

⑤ Type a name for the command.

⑥ Click **OK**.

Dreamweaver saves the command.

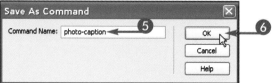

Note: *You cannot use this feature with all commands. For example, clicking and dragging an element cannot be included in a command.*

APPLY THE COMMAND

1 Select the element to which you want to apply the command.

2 Click **Commands**.

3 Click the command that you want to apply.

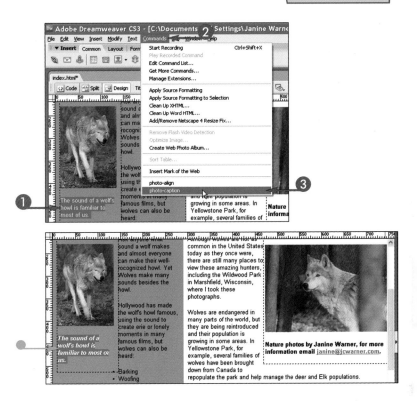

● Dreamweaver applies the command to the selection.

TIPS

How do I change the name of a custom command?

1 Click **Commands**.

2 Click **Edit Command List**.

3 Click a command, and type a new name.

4 Click **Close**.

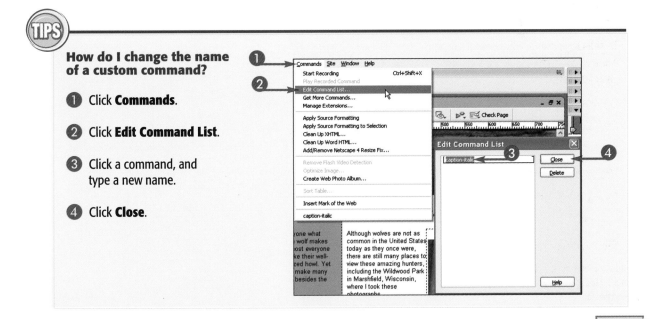

Set Preferences

You can easily change the default appearance and behavior of Dreamweaver by specifying settings in the Preferences dialog box. This enables you to modify the user interface of Dreamweaver to better suit how you like to work.

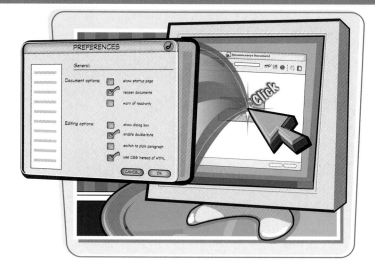

① Click **Edit**.

② Click **Preferences**.

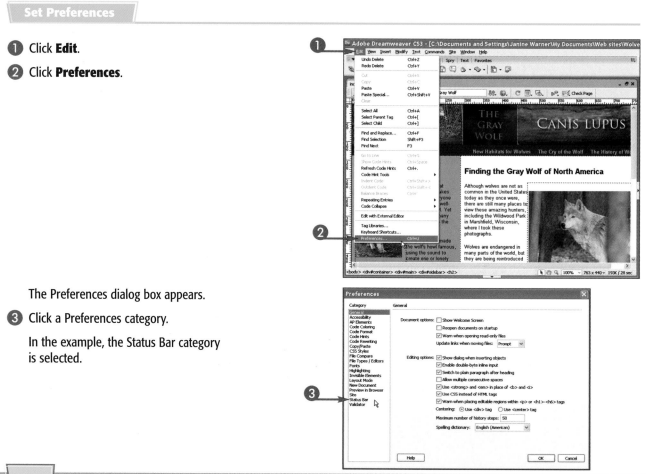

The Preferences dialog box appears.

③ Click a Preferences category.

In the example, the Status Bar category is selected.

● Options appear for the category that you selected.

④ Change settings for the property that you want to alter.

● In this example, the Connection Speed option is set to 128K.

⑤ Click **OK**.

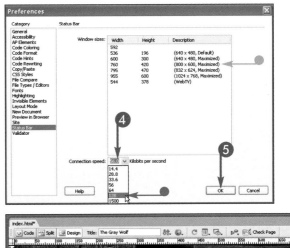

The changes take effect immediately.

● In this example, the status bar now displays download times that assume a 128K connection speed.

TIP

How do I ensure that Dreamweaver does not change my HTML or other code?

You can select options under the Code Rewriting category in the Preferences dialog box to ensure that Dreamweaver does not automatically correct or modify your code. For example, you can turn off the error-correcting functions, specify the files that it should not rewrite based on file extension, or disable the character-encoding features.

Working with HTML

Dreamweaver helps you to build Web pages by automatically writing the HTML code as you create pages in Design view. This chapter introduces the code behind your pages, as well as the tools in Dreamweaver that enable you to edit HTML code.

Although Dreamweaver writes the HTML code for you and saves you time, you always have the option of writing or editing the code manually.

XHTML

Extensible Hypertext Markup Language (XHTML) is the formatting language that you can use to create Web pages. When you open a Web page in a Web browser, the XHTML code tells the Web browser how to display the text, images, and other content on the page. By default, Dreamweaver CS3 writes XHTML instead of HTML because XHTML is a stricter version of HTML that is designed to comply with contemporary Web standards.

XHTML Tags

The basic unit of XHTML is called a tag. You can recognize XHTML tags by their angle brackets:

`<h1>This is a headline</h1>`

`<p>It is followed by some plain text in a paragraph tag. <b>This text will appear bold because it is surrounded by the bold tag.</b> This text will not be bold.</p>`

You can format text and other elements on your page by placing them inside the XHTML tags.

How Tags Work

Some XHTML tags work in pairs. Open and close tags surround content in a document and control the formatting of the content, such as when the `<b>` and `</b>` tags set off bold text. Other tags can stand alone, such as the `<br>` tag, which adds a line break. In general, XHTML tags must have a closing tag, even if there is only one tag, and close tags always contain a forward slash (/). As a result, the line break tag in XHTML looks like this: `<br />`. XHTML must be written in lowercase letters.

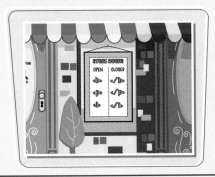

Create Web Pages without Knowing HTML

Dreamweaver streamlines the process of creating Web pages by giving you an easy-to-use, visual interface with which you can generate XHTML code. You specify formatting with menu commands and button clicks, and Dreamweaver takes care of writing the underlying XHTML code. When you build a Web page in the Document window, you can see your page as it will appear in a Web browser, instead of as XHTML code.

XHTML Documents

Because XHTML documents are plain-text files, you can open and edit them with any text editor. In fact, in the early days of the Web, most people created their pages with simple editors such as Notepad (in Windows) and SimpleText (in Macintosh). If you use Dreamweaver, you have the advantage of being able to write XHTML code when you want to, or letting Dreamweaver write it for you.

Direct Access to the XHTML Code

Dreamweaver allows you direct access to the raw XHTML code. This is helpful if you want to edit the code directly. In Dreamweaver, you can work in Code view, Design view, or Split view, which enables you to see Code and Design views simultaneously. You can also use the Quick Tag Editor to edit code without switching to Code or Design view.

Work in Design View and Code View

You can switch to Code view in the Document window to inspect and edit the XHTML code and other code on the Web page. You can use the Split view to see both the XHTML code and Design view at the same time.

You will probably do most of your work in Design view, which displays your page approximately as it will appear in a Web browser.

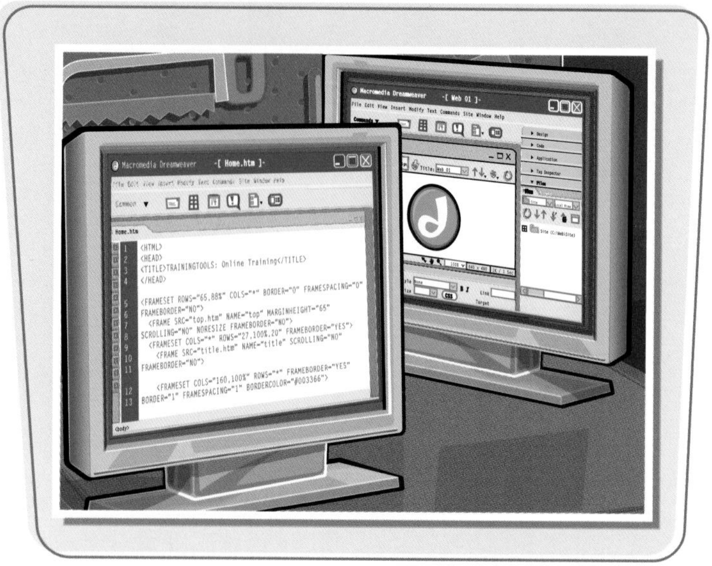

Work in Design View and Code View

1. In the Document window, click the **Split** view button (Split).

- You can click the **Code** view button (Code) to display the source code of your page in the Document window.
- You can click the **Design** view button (Design) to hide the code and only view the page design as it would appear in a Web browser.

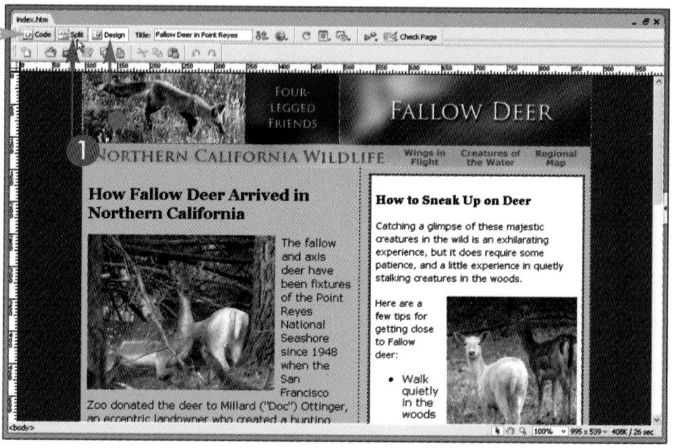

Both Code view and Design view appear in the Document window when you click Split.

- The XHTML and other code appear in upper pane.
- The Design view appears in the lower pane.

2. Click to select some text in the Design view pane.

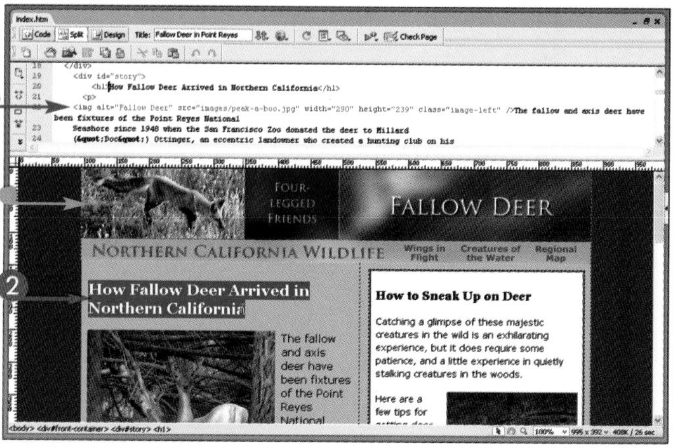

● The corresponding code becomes highlighted in the Code view pane.

③ Type to edit the text in the Design view pane.

● The text automatically updates in the corresponding code.

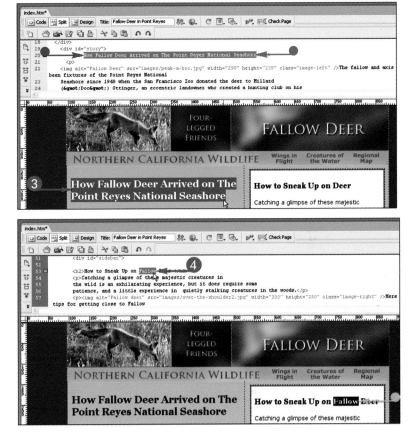

④ Click in the Code view pane and type to make changes.

● The content in the Design view pane updates as you make your changes.

TIP

How do I turn on line numbers in Code view or make code wrap at the right edge of the window?

You can access both of these options, as well as others, by clicking the Options button at the top of the Document window when you are in Code view.

Word Wrap
Line Number
Highlight Invalid
Syntax Coloring
Auto Indent

Every XHTML document contains head and body tags. To view the XHTML code of a Web page, you can click the Code view button in the Document window, or you can click Window and then click Code Inspector.

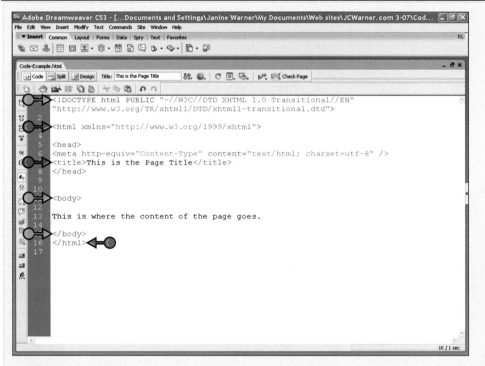

DOCTYPE

The DOCTYPE describes the document and identifies that it was created with XHTML 1.0 Transitional, which is currently recommended for most Web pages.

`<html>` Tags

Open and close `<html>` tags begin and end every HTML document.

`<title>` Tags

Open and close `<title>` tags display the content that appears in the title bar of a Web browser.

`<body>` Tags

All of the content that displays in the Web browser window is contained within the open and close `<body>` tags.

XHTML is made up of many different HTML tags, each designed to specify a particular kind of formatting, such as paragraph breaks, headline styles, and bulleted lists.

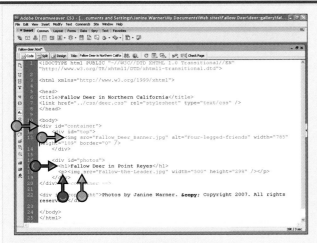

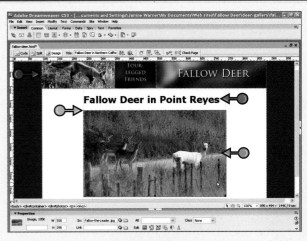

Code View

This page is displayed in Code view in Dreamweaver.

`<div>` Tag

The `<div>` tag is used to divide content, and is often combined with styles that are created in CSS.

`<h1>` to `<h6>` Tags

The heading tags are ideal for formatting headlines. The `<h1>` tag creates the largest heading style, while the `<h6>` tag is the smallest.

`<p>` Tag

The open and close `<p>` tags separate paragraphs of content and add a space between images and other elements.

`<img src>` Tag

The `<img src>` tag is used to insert an image into a page.

Design View

This is the same page displayed in Design view.

`<div>` Tag

The `<div>` tag creates a container for the content. The width and centering of the container are defined with a CSS style.

`<h1>` to `<h6>` Tags

The `<h1>` tag makes the headline text large and bold.

`<p>` Tag

The `<p>` tag separates content into paragraph blocks and ads space around images and other elements.

`<img src>` Tag

The `<img src>` tag displays the image on the page.

Clean Up HTML Code

Dreamweaver can optimize the code in your Web pages by deleting redundant or non-functional tags. This can decrease the page file size and make the source code easier to read in Code view.

It's easy to create unused tags when you do things such as copy and paste content. To keep formatting more consistent, it's a good idea to delete unused tags by running the Clean Up HTML command.

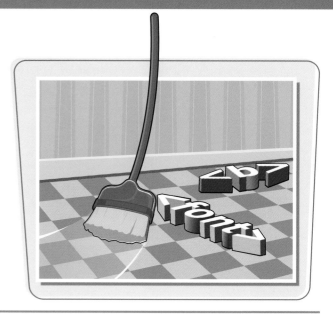

Clean Up HTML Code

① Click **Split** to display the Code view and Design view at the same time.

● In this example, there is an empty `<h1>` tag.

● Multiple `<font>` tags appear, adding unnecessary code.

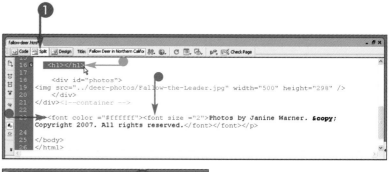

② Click **Commands**.

③ Click **Clean Up XHTML**.

The Clean Up HTML/XHTML dialog box appears.

④ Click the clean-up options for code that you want to remove (☐ changes to ✓).

⑤ Click the clean-up options that you want to select (☐ changes to ✓).

⑥ Click **OK**.

● Dreamweaver parses the HTML code and displays the results, including a summary of what was removed.

⑦ Click **OK**.

● The cleaned-up HTML code appears in the Document window.

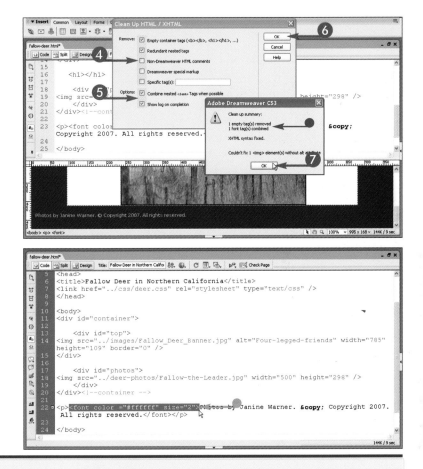

TIPS

How do empty tags end up appearing in the Dreamweaver HTML code?

Sometimes you may heavily edit Web-page text in the Document window, for example, by cutting and pasting sentences and reformatting words. In these cases, Dreamweaver inadvertently removes text from within tags without removing the actual tags.

Does Dreamweaver fix invalid HTML code?

By default, Dreamweaver rewrites some instances of invalid HTML code. When you open an HTML document, Dreamweaver rewrites tags that are not nested properly, closes tags that are not allowed to remain open, and removes extra closing tags. If Dreamweaver does not recognize a tag, it highlights it in red and displays it in the Document window, but it does not remove the tag. You can change or turn off this behavior by clicking **Edit**, then clicking **Preferences**, and then selecting the category **Code Rewriting**.

Dreamweaver gives you various ways to view, add to, and edit the head content of a Web page. For example, MetaTags store special descriptive information about the page that can be used by search engines.

INSERT META KEYWORDS

1. Click **Insert**.
2. Click **HTML**.
3. Click **Head Tags**.
4. Click **Keywords**.

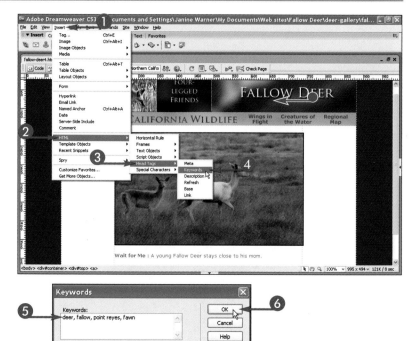

The Keywords dialog box appears.

5. Type a series of keywords, separated by commas, that describe the content of the page.
6. Click **OK**.

INSERT META DESCRIPTION

1 Click **Insert**.

2 Click **HTML**.

3 Click **Head Tags**.

4 Click **Description**.

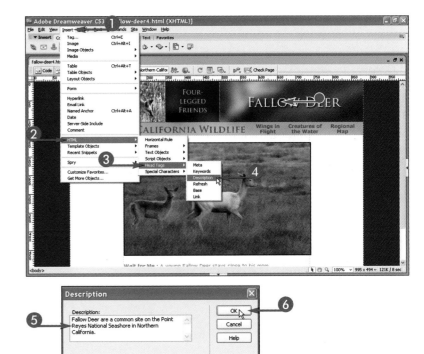

The Description dialog box appears.

5 Type a brief description of the content of the page.

6 Click **OK**.

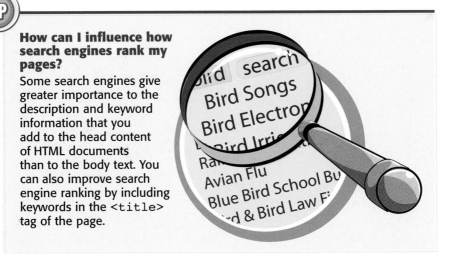

TIP

How can I influence how search engines rank my pages?

Some search engines give greater importance to the description and keyword information that you add to the head content of HTML documents than to the body text. You can also improve search engine ranking by including keywords in the `<title>` tag of the page.

Access Reference Information About HTML Tags

You can get quick access to reference information about HTML tags and their attributes by using the Reference tab in the Code panel. You can also insert short pieces of prewritten HTML code from the Snippets panel.

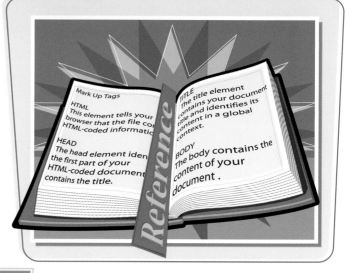

Access Reference Information About HTML Tags

USE THE REFERENCE PANEL

1 Click ⬚ Split to display both Design view and Code view.

2 Click and drag to select an HTML tag.

Note: It is not necessary to select the entire tag.

3 Click **Window**.

4 Click **Reference**.

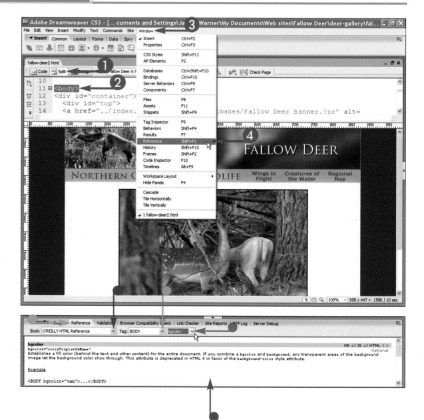

● The Reference panel opens, displaying a description of the HTML tag.

● You can click here and select a tag attribute.

● Information appears on the attribute.

● You can click here to look up a different HTML tag.

● You can click here to find information about other technologies, such as JavaScript and CSS.

CLOSE PANEL GROUPS

1 In the top-left corner of the Property inspector, right-click here.

2 Click **Close panel group**.

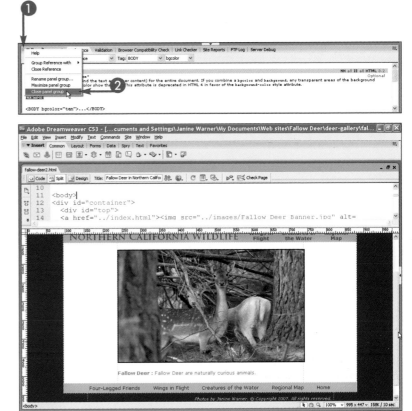

The panel group at the bottom of the page closes.

Panels take up a lot of the design area, so closing them when you are not using them gives you more design space in Dreamweaver.

TIPS

Does Dreamweaver support all of the tags listed in the Reference tab?

Yes, but you will not find buttons or menus that include every tag you can possibly create with Dreamweaver. That is one of the reasons the reference is so valuable. You can always write your own tags in Code view if you know what the tags are. To use the reference command, just click the down arrow next to the Book text box in the Reference panel. The drop-down list displays references for many other technologies, as well, including CSS, JavaScript, and XML.

What does the text *Lorem ipsum dolor* mean that appears in Web pages?

The text is Latin, a commonly used language for "dummy" text that is used as a placeholder when laying out pages. Although Latin text is often used as placeholder text in designs, its meaning generally has nothing to do with its usage. The idea is that using Latin text will make it obvious that the text still needs to be replaced.

5

Formatting and Styling Text

Text is the easiest type of information to add to a Web page using Dreamweaver. This chapter shows you how to create headlines, paragraphs, bulleted lists, and stylized text.

When you format text with heading tags, you can create large, bold text and specify a range of sizes. You can also align your heading text.

Create a Heading

① Click and drag to select the text.

② Click the **Format** ⊡.

③ Click a heading level.

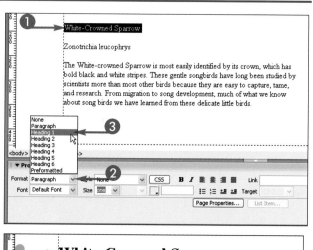

● The font size is larger, and the text is now bold. White space separates it from other text.

④ Click and drag to select more text.

⑤ Click the **Format** ⊡.

⑥ Click a different heading level.

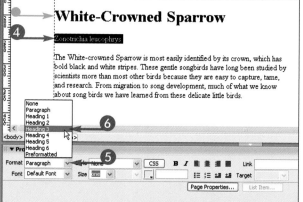

● The second heading appears different from the first, but still bold.

Note: *The higher the heading number, the smaller the text formatting.*

⑦ Click and drag to select the heading text.

⑧ Click an alignment option to align your heading.

You can choose to align left (▤), center (▤), align right (▤), or justify (▤).

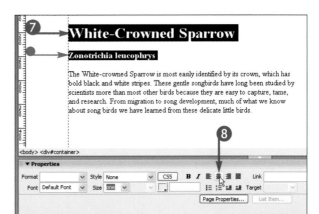

The heading text aligns on the page.

What heading levels should I use to format my text?

Headings 1, 2, and 3 are often used for titles and subtitles. Heading 4 is similar to a bold version of default text. Headings 5 and 6 are often used for smaller text, such as copyright or disclaimer information.

Why are my headlines different sizes when I see them on another computer?

Size can vary from one computer to the next, and some users set their Web browsers to display larger or smaller type on their computer. Browsers use the default text size to determine the size of the heading. For example, Heading 1 text is three times larger than the default text size, and Heading 6 text is one-third the default size.

Create
Paragraphs

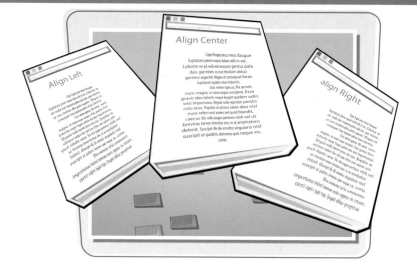

You can organize text on your Web page by creating and aligning paragraphs.

Create Paragraphs

1 Type the text for your Web page into the Document window.

2 Position the cursor where you want a paragraph break.

3 Press **Enter** (**Return**).

● A blank line appears between the blocks of text, separating the text into paragraphs.

Note: *Paragraphs align left by default.*

④ Click and drag to select the paragraph that you want to align.

⑤ Click an alignment option to align your paragraph.

You can choose to align left (≡), center (≡), align right (≡), or justify (≡).

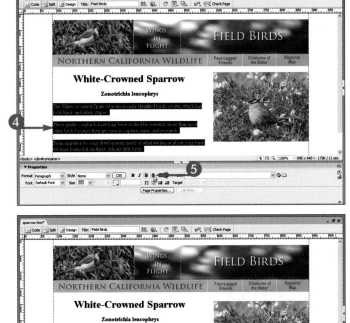

● The paragraph aligns on the page.

TIPS

What controls the width of the paragraphs on my Web page?

The width of your paragraphs depends on the width of the Web browser window or the container that surrounds your text. When a user changes the size of the browser window, the widths of the paragraphs also change. You can also use tables or CSS to create containers and further control the width of your paragraphs. For more information on tables, see Chapter 8. For more information on CSS, see Chapter 13.

What is the HTML code for paragraphs?

In HTML, paragraphs are distinguished by opening `<p>` and closing `</p>` tags. You can click the **Code view** button (⬚ Code) to view the HTML code of the page.

When you do not want a full paragraph break, you can use line breaks to keep lines of text adjacent. When you hold down the Shift key and press Enter (Return), you create a line break.

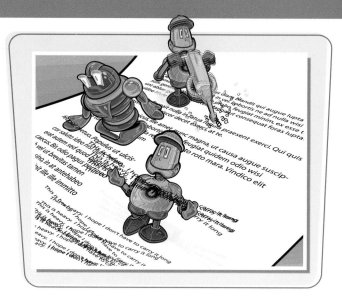

Create Line Breaks

1 Click where you want the line of text to break.

2 Press `Shift` + `Enter` (`Shift` + `Return`).

● Dreamweaver adds a line break.

Note: *You can combine paragraph and line breaks to add more space between lines of text.*

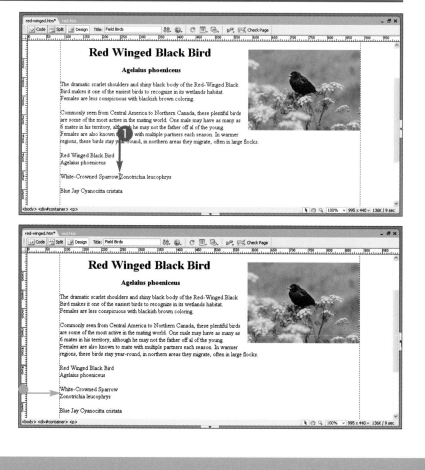

Indent Paragraphs

You can make selected paragraphs stand out from the rest of the text on your Web page by indenting them. For example, indents are often used for displaying quotations.

Indent Paragraphs

① Click and drag to select a paragraph.

② Click 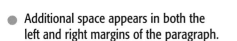 to indent the text.

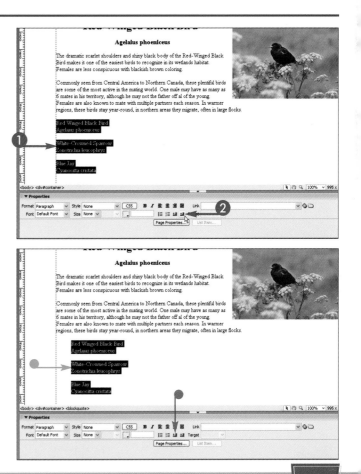

● Additional space appears in both the left and right margins of the paragraph.

You can repeat Steps **1** and **2** to indent a paragraph further.

● You can outdent an indented paragraph by clicking ⊒.

You can organize text items into ordered and unordered lists. Unordered lists have items that are indented and bulleted, but, unlike ordered lists, they are not listed by numbers or letters.

Create Lists

CREATE AN UNORDERED LIST

1. Type your list items into the Document window.

2. Click between the items and press **Enter** (**Return**) to place each item in a separate paragraph.

3. Click and drag to select all of the list items.

4. Click **Unordered List** (☰) in the Property inspector.

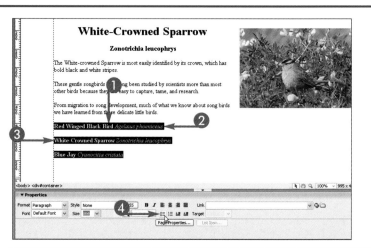

- The list items appear indented and bulleted.

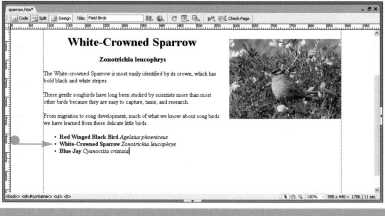

CREATE ORDERED LISTS

1. Type your list items into the Document window.

2. Click between the items and press Enter (Return) to place each item in a separate paragraph.

3. Click and drag to select all of the list items.

4. Click **Ordered List** (icon) in the Property inspector.

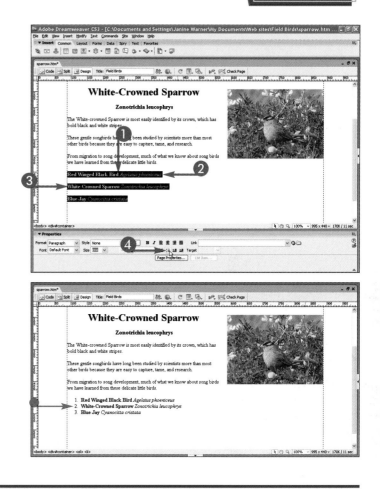

● The list items appear indented and numbered.

TIPS

Can I modify the appearance of my unordered list?

Yes. You can modify the style of an unordered list by highlighting an item in the list and clicking **Text**, then clicking **List**, and then clicking **Properties**. The dialog box that appears enables you to select different bullet styles for your unordered list.

Can I modify the appearance of my ordered list?

Yes. You can modify the style of an ordered list by highlighting an item in the list and clicking **Text**, then clicking **List**, and then clicking **Properties**. The dialog box that appears enables you to select different numbering schemes for your ordered list.

Insert Special Characters

You can insert special characters into your Web page that do not appear on your keyboard.

INSERT CHARACTERS

1 Click the **Text** tab in the **Insert** bar.

2 Click where you want to insert the special character.

3 Click the **Characters** button (🖼).

4 Click the special character that you want to insert.

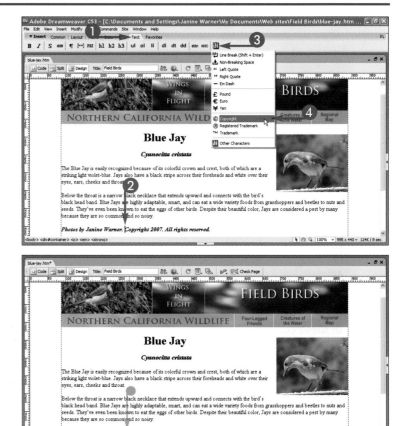

● The special character appears in your Web page text.

INSERT OTHER CHARACTERS

1 Click where you want to insert the special character.

2 Click the icon at the top of the Characters menu.

Note: *The character at the top of the menu changes to represent on the last character selected.*

3 Click **Other Characters** ().

The Insert Other Character dialog box appears, displaying a wider variety of special characters.

4 Click a special character.

The HTML code that defines that special character is inserted into the HTML code of the page.

5 Click **OK**.

● The special character appears in your Web page text.

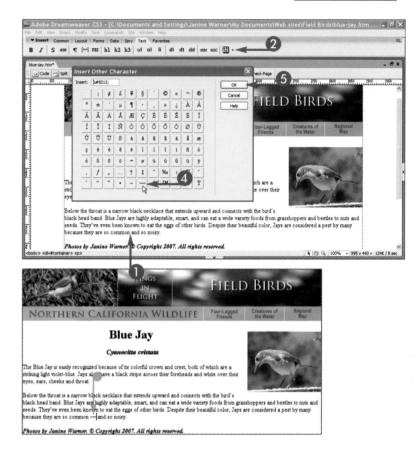

TIPS

How do I include non-English-language text on my Web page?

Many foreign languages feature accented characters that do not appear on standard keyboards. You can insert most of these characters using the special characters feature described in this task.

Why do special characters look strange in a Web browser?

Although most Web browsers display double quotation marks without problems, some standard punctuation marks are considered special characters and require special code. If you do not use the special HTML code, those characters may not display properly.

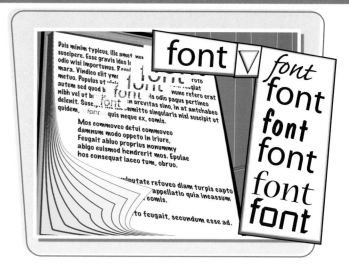

For aesthetic purposes or to emphasize certain elements on your Web pages, you can change the font style of your text.

You can customize the fonts on your Web pages by using style sheets, also called Cascading Style Sheets or CSS. For more information about style sheets, see Chapters 12 and 13.

Change the Font Face

CHANGE THE FONT

1. Click and drag to select the text.

2. Click the **Font** ☑ in the Property inspector.

3. Click a font collection.

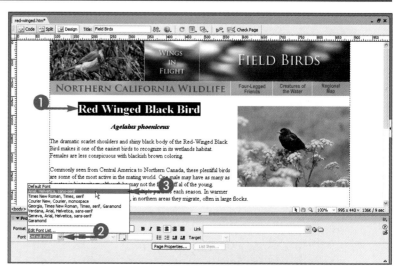

● The text changes to the first font in the collection that is available on your hard drive.

You can create a new style in Dreamweaver and apply it by using the Property inspector.

Note: To find out how to create styles, see Chapter 12.

ADD AN ENTRY TO THE FONT MENU

1 Click **Text**.

2 Click **Font**.

3 Click **Edit Font List**.

The Edit Font List dialog box appears.

● The fonts that appear in the Font menu display in this area.

● The fonts installed on your computer appear in the Available Fonts list.

4 Click a font.

5 Click the **Add Font arrows** button () to add the font.

6 Click **OK**.

● The new font appears in the Font menu.

How are fonts classified?

The two most common categories of fonts are serif and sans-serif. Serif fonts are distinguished by the decorations, or serifs, that make the ends of their lines curly. Common serif fonts include Times New Roman, Palatino, and Garamond. Sans-serif fonts lack these decorations and have straight edges. Common sans-serif fonts include Arial, Verdana, and Helvetica.

Why are there so few fonts available from the Font menu?

A font must be installed on the user's computer to display in a Web browser. Dreamweaver's default list of fonts specifies the common typefaces that are available on most computers, and alternate styles if the user does not have those fonts installed. If you want to use an unusual font, then you should convert the text to a graphic.

Change the Font Size

You can change the size of your text by using the font size tag. Unlike the heading tags, when you apply the font size tag, Dreamweaver does not add a paragraph return.

Change the Font Size

1 Click and drag to select the text.

2 Click the **Size** ⏷.

3 Click a font size.

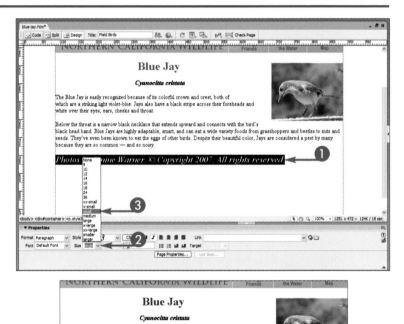

● The size of the text changes.

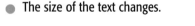

You can change the color of text on all or part of your Web page. You should ensure that it is readable and complements the background.

Change the Font Color

1 Click and drag to select the text that you want to change.

2 Click the **Color Swatch** 🔲 in the Property inspector (⌖ changes to 🖋).

The Color Palette appears.

3 Click a color.

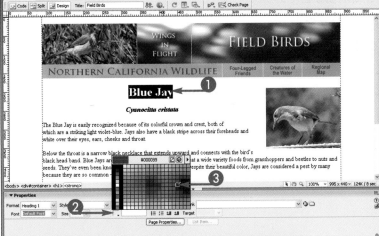

● The selected text appears in the new color.

Change Text and Page Colors

You can change text and background colors for the entire page in the Page Properties dialog box.

① Click **Modify**.

② Click **Page Properties**.

● You can also click the **Page Properties** button in the Property inspector.

The Page Properties dialog box appears.

③ Click the **Background Color Swatch** 🔲.

The Color Palette appears.

④ Click any color to select it.

⑤ Click **Apply** to see the color change on the page.

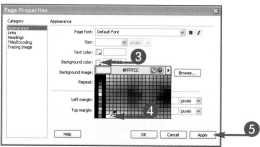

⑥ Click the **Text Color Swatch** 🔲.

The Color Palette appears.

⑦ Click any color to select it.

⑧ Click **Apply**.

⑨ Click **OK** to close the dialog box.

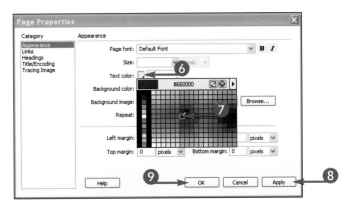

Your text appears in the new color on your Web page.

TIP

What are the letter and number combinations that appear in the color fields of Dreamweaver?

HTML represents colors using six-digit codes called hexadecimal codes, or hex codes. These codes represent the amount of red, green, and blue that is used to create a particular color, and are preceded by a pound sign (#). Instead of ranging from 0 to 9, hex-code digits range from 0 to F, with A equal to 10, B equal to 11, and so on through F, which is equal to 15. The first two digits in the hex code specify the amount of red in the selected color. The second two digits specify the amount of green, and the third two digits specify the amount of blue.

Copy Text from Another Document

You can save time by copying and pasting text from an existing document, instead of typing it all over again. This is particularly convenient when you have tabular data that needs to appear in a table or a lot of text in a word processing program such as Microsoft Word. When you paste text in Dreamweaver, you have multiple formatting choices.

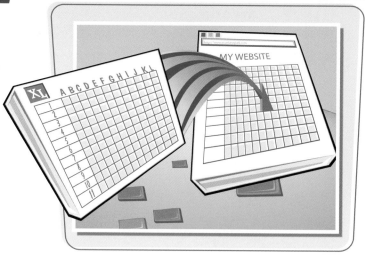

Copy Text from Another Document

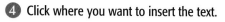

① Click and drag to select text in the original file, such as this document created in Microsoft Word.

② Click **Edit**.

③ Click **Copy**.

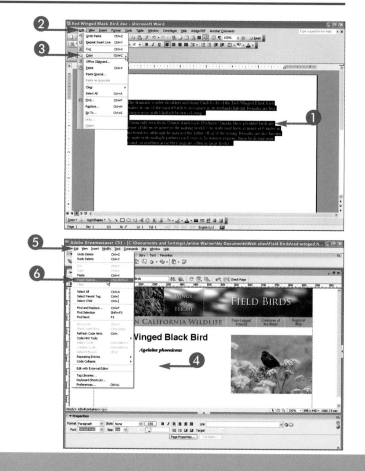

④ Click where you want to insert the text.

⑤ Click **Edit**.

⑥ Click **Paste Special**.

The Paste Special dialog box appears.

7 Click a **Paste** option.

8 Click **OK**.

The text is inserted into the HTML file.

Dreamweaver automatically formats the text in HTML, based on the formatting option that you selected in the Paste Special dialog box.

Red Winged Black Bird

Agelaius phoeniceus

The dramatic scarlet shoulders and shiny black body of the Red-Winged Black Bird makes it one of the easiest birds to recognize in its wetlands habitat. Females are less conspicuous with blackish brown coloring.

Commonly seen from Central America to Northern Canada, these plentiful birds are some of the most active in the mating world. One male may have as many as 6 mates in his territory, although he may not be the father off al of the young. Females are also known to mate with multiple partners each season. In warmer regions, these birds stay year-round, in northern areas they migrate, often in large flocks.

TIP

When is it a good idea to copy and paste text?
Even if you type at speeds of over 100 words per minute, you can save time if you do not have to retype all of your documents. If your original text file was created using a word processing program such as Microsoft Word, then you can speed up the process by importing the Word document into Dreamweaver. You can also copy and paste text from Excel documents, and Dreamweaver automatically builds tables to duplicate the formatting from Excel. Once you have pasted the content into Dreamweaver, you can edit and format the text or other data as you normally would.

CHAPTER

6

Working with Images and Multimedia

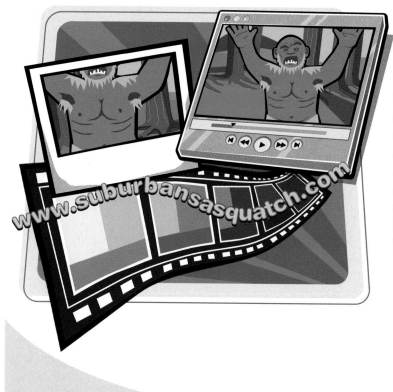

You can make your Web page much more interesting by adding digital photos, scanned art, animation, video, and other visual elements. This chapter shows you how to insert and format these elements.

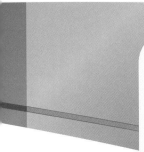

Insert an Image into a Web Page

You can insert different types of images into your Web page, including clip art, digital camera images, and scanned photos. You must first save the images in a Web format, such as GIF, PNG, or JPEG.

Insert an Image into a Web Page

① Click to position the mouse (⇖) where you want to insert the image.

② Click **Insert**.

③ Click **Image**.

You can also click **Image** (▣) in the Common Insert bar.

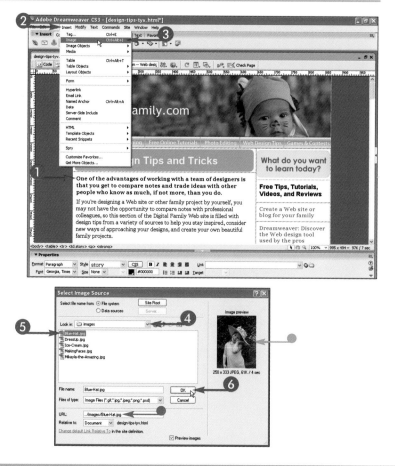

The Select Image Source dialog box appears.

④ Click here and select the folder that contains the image.

⑤ Click the image file that you want to insert into your Web page.

● A preview of the image appears.

● You can insert an image that exists at an external Web address by typing the address into the URL field.

⑥ Click **OK**.

The Image Tag Accessibility Attributes dialog box appears.

7 Enter a description of the image.

8 Enter a URL for a longer description, if available.

Alternate text appears in the code behind an image and displays only if the image is not visible. Alternate text is especially important for the visually impaired visitors who use screen readers to "read" Web pages to them.

● The image appears where you positioned your cursor in the Web page.

To delete an image, click the image and press Delete.

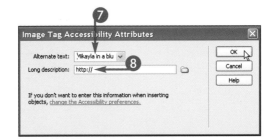

TIP

What file formats can you use for Web images?
The majority of the images that you see on Web pages are GIF and JPEG files. Both GIF and JPEG are compressed file formats, which means that they are smaller than other image files and therefore download faster. The GIF format is best for images that have a limited number of colors, such as cartoons or line art. The JPEG format is best for photographs and other images with millions of colors. You can insert both GIF and JPEG files into your Web page using the steps described in this task.

Wrap Text Around an Image

You can wrap text around an image by aligning the image to one side of a Web page. Wrapping text around images enables you to fit more information onto the screen, and gives your Web pages a more finished, professional look. There are many alignment options, and you may want to experiment to find the best effect for your page.

Wrap Text Around an Image

ALIGN AN IMAGE

① Click an image to select it.

② Click the **Align** ▽.

③ Click an alignment option to position the image.

● You can click the ▽ to expand the Property inspector if the alignment options are not visible.

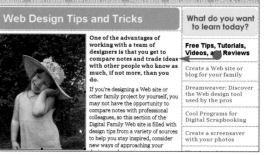

● The text flows around the image according to the alignment that you selected.

In this example, the text flows to the right of the left-aligned image.

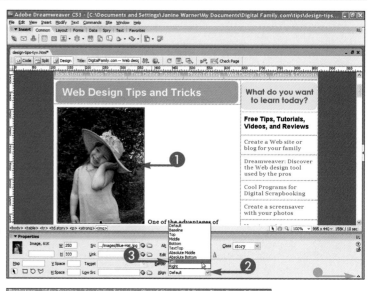

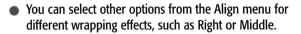

- You can select other options from the Align menu for different wrapping effects, such as Right or Middle.

- In this example, the text flows to the left of the right-aligned image.

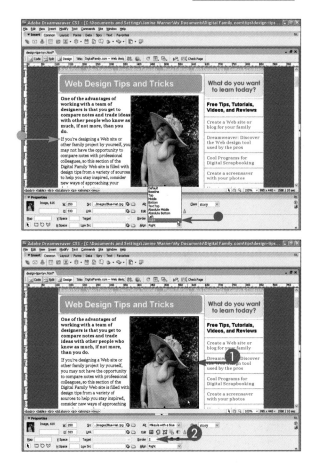

ADD A BORDER TO AN IMAGE

1 Click an image to select it.

2 Type the width into the Border field.

This example uses a border of 2 pixels.

A black border appears around the image. If the image is a link, the border appears in the link color.

Note: To learn how to change link colors, see Chapter 7.

TIPS

How can I determine the download time for my Web page?

The total size of your Web page appears in kilobytes (K) on the status bar. The total size includes the size of your HTML file, the size of your images, and the size of any other elements on the Web page. Next to the size is the estimated download time for the Web page.

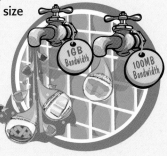

What is the ideal size of a Web page?

Most Web designers feel comfortable putting up a page with a total size under 100K. However, there are exceptions to this rule. For example, you may want to break this rule for an especially important image file. The 100K limit does not apply to multimedia files, although multimedia files should be kept as small as possible.

Align an Image

The alignment of an image can give a photo or banner prominence on your Web page. Depending on the layout of your Web page, you can center an image or align it left or right.

1. Click to place the cursor to the right of the image.

2. Press Enter (Return) to place the image on its own line.

3. Click and drag to select an image and text at the same time.

4. Click 🖹.

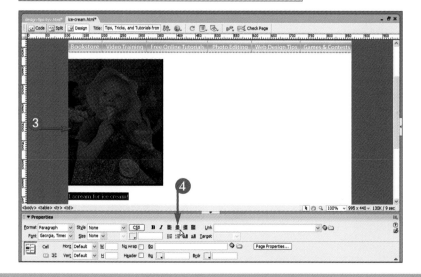

● The image and text appear in the center of the page.

● You can align the image and text to the right side of the page by clicking 🖹, or align the image to the left side by clicking 🖹.

● Using the alignment tools to align the image does not influence the text wrapping around the image.

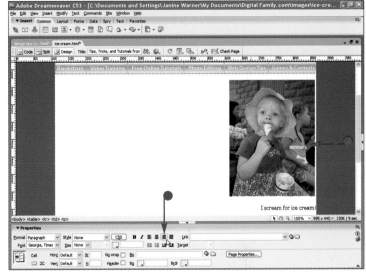

How can I use centered images to enhance my text?

You can create custom graphics or icons in an image-editing program, and then use these images as visual elements on your Web page. You can use small, centered icons to divide main sections of text in your Web page. These icons serve the same purpose as horizontal rules, but add a more sophisticated look to your Web pages.

Crop an Image

You can trim, or crop, an image by using the Crop tool and dragging the crop handles to adjust how much of the image you want to show. This can be useful for quick edits without using an external image-editing program, as it physically crops the image file.

Crop an Image

1 Click an image to select it.

2 Click the **Crop** tool (⬚).

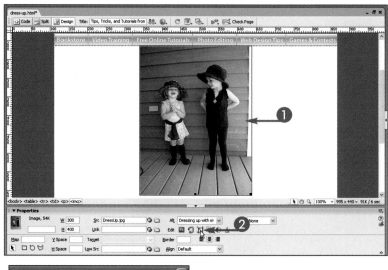

A dialog box appears.

● You can turn off this warning by checking the option box (☐ changes to ☑).

3 Click **OK**.

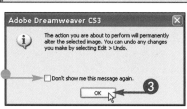

④ Click and drag the black, square handles to define the area that you want to crop.

The part of the photo that appears grayed out will be deleted.

⑤ Double-click inside the crop box.

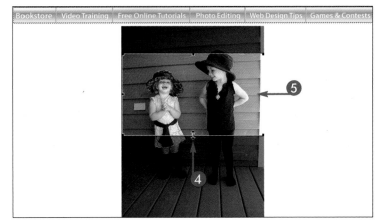

● The image trims to the size of the crop box.

Note: *Keep in mind that when you save the page, the image is permanently cropped.*

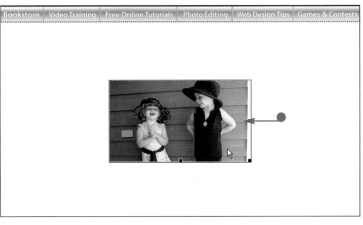

TIP

Should I edit images in Dreamweaver or use an external graphics program?

Adobe has added the Crop and other basic editing tools to make working on a Web page faster and easier. If you need to do a simple crop, the Crop tool is faster than opening the image in an image-editing program such as Adobe Fireworks or Adobe Photoshop. However, if you want to save a copy of the original before you make the crop, or do other image editing, then you need to use a dedicated image-editing program.

Resize an Image

You can change the display size of an image without changing the file size of the image. You can do this by using a percentage or a pixel size, or by clicking and dragging the corner of the image.

Pixels are tiny, solid-color squares that make up a digital image. When you specify a size in pixels, you are using a very small unit of measurement.

Resize an Image

RESIZE USING PIXEL OR PERCENTAGE DIMENSIONS

1 Click an image to select it.

● The dimensions of the image appear.

2 Type the desired width of the image, either in pixels or as a percentage.

Instead of pixels, you can type a percentage of the window or table cell for the width and height. For example, you can type **50%** in both fields to make the image half the size of the window or table cell.

3 Press Enter (Return).

4 Type the desired height of the image in pixels or as a percentage.

5 Press Enter (Return).

● The image displays with its new dimensions.

CLICK AND DRAG TO RESIZE

① Click an image to select it.

② Drag one of the handles at the edge of the image (changes to).

To resize the image proportionally, press and hold down **Shift** as you drag a corner.

The image expands or contracts to the new size.

RESET THE IMAGE TO THE ORIGINAL SIZE

You can reset any image to its original size.

① Click the image to select it.

② Click **Reset Size** ( ) in the Property inspector.

The image returns to its original size.

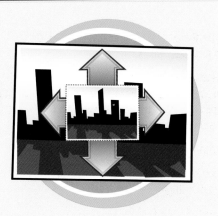

What is the best way to change the dimensions of an image on a Web page?

Although you can change the pixel dimensions or click and drag an image in Dreamweaver to stretch or shrink it on the Web page, this does not actually resize the image's true dimensions. Clicking and dragging an image may cause distortion or alter proportions. A better way to resize an image is to open it in an image editor such as Adobe Fireworks or Photoshop, and change its actual size.

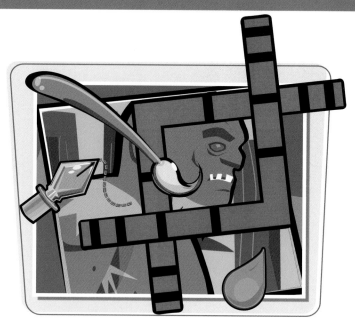

Adobe designed Dreamweaver to work with multiple image programs so that you can easily open and edit images while you are working on your Web pages. Adobe Fireworks and Photoshop are sophisticated image-editing programs that are designed to make many changes to an image.

Although you can use any image editor, Fireworks and Photoshop are integrated with Dreamweaver because Adobe makes both programs.

Open an Image in an Image Editor

① Click an image to select it in Dreamweaver.

You can open any image in an external image editor from within Dreamweaver.

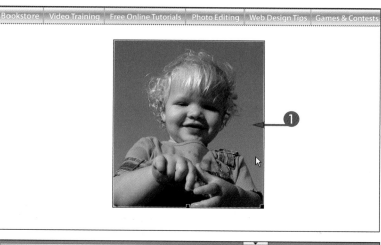

② Click **Photoshop** (▣) in the Property inspector.

You may have to wait a few moments while Photoshop opens.

In Dreamweaver's preferences, you can associate other image editors, such as Adobe Fireworks.

The image opens in the Photoshop window.

You can now edit the image.

3 Click **File**.

4 Click **Save As** and save the image with the same name and format, replacing the original image.

Your changes to the image become permanent.

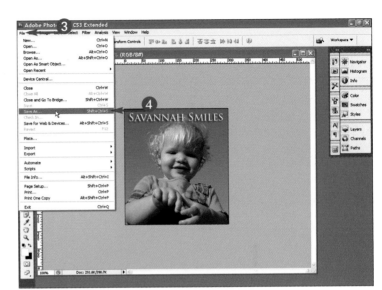

● Photoshop saves the image and it automatically updates in the Dreamweaver window.

To edit the image again or to edit another image, you can select the image and repeat Steps **2** to **4**.

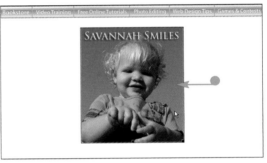

What can you do in an image-editing program?

A program such as Adobe Fireworks or Photoshop allows you to edit and combine images to create almost anything that you can imagine. If you have Fireworks installed, then you can open it to edit an image directly from Dreamweaver. In the Property inspector, click the **Edit/Fireworks Logo** button (or 🖼 if you use Photoshop).

Add Space Around an Image

You can add space around an image to separate it from the text and other images on your Web page. This creates a cleaner page layout.

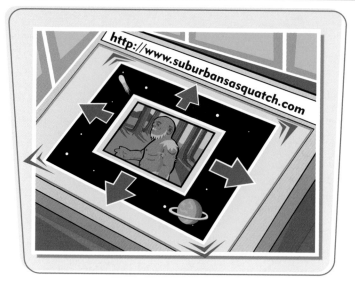

Add Space Around an Image

ADD SPACE TO THE LEFT AND RIGHT OF AN IMAGE

1. Click an image to select it.

2. Type an amount in the H Space field.

3. Press Enter (Return).

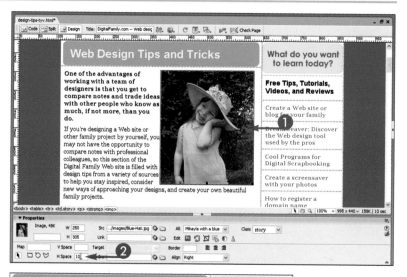

● Extra space appears to the left and right of the image.

ADD SPACE ABOVE AND BELOW AN IMAGE

1 Click the image to select it.

2 Type an amount in the V Space field.

3 Press Enter (Return).

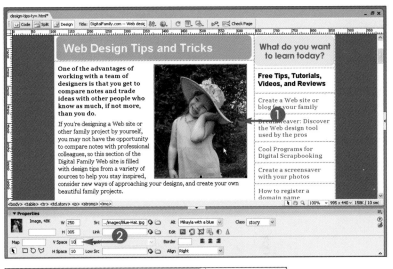

● Extra space appears above and below the image.

TIP

Is there any other way to add space around my image?
In many cases, adding space around your images enhances the appearance of your Web page. The extra space makes text easier to read and keeps adjacent images from appearing as a single image. However, when you add space using the horizontal and vertical space options in Dreamweaver, you add space to all sides of the image. If you only want to create space on one side, you can create a style using CSS margin settings to add space to only one side. You learn more about CSS in Chapters 12 and 13.

Add a Background Image

You can incorporate a background image to add texture to your Web page. Background images appear beneath any text or images that are on your Web page, and are repeated across and down the Web browser window.

Add a Background Image

① Click **Page Properties** in the Property inspector.

The Page Properties dialog box appears.

② Click **Appearance**.

③ Click **Browse**.

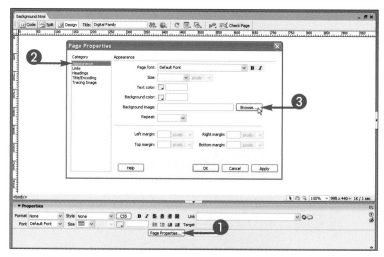

The Select Image Source dialog box appears.

④ Click here and select the folder that contains the background image file.

⑤ Click the background image that you want to insert.

● A preview image appears.

⑥ Click **OK**.

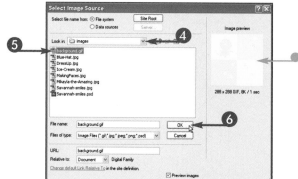

● The image filename and path appear in the Background image text field.

⑦ Click **OK**.

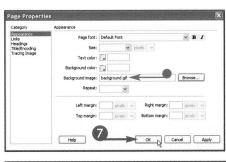

The image appears as a background on the Web page.

Note: *If the image is smaller than the display area, as in this example, it tiles horizontally and vertically to fill the entire window. You can resize the image in an image editor to adjust its appearance.*

TIPS

What types of images make good backgrounds?

Textures, subtle patterns, and photos with large open areas all make good background images. It is important to make sure that the image does not clash with the text and other content in the foreground, or overwhelm the rest of the page. Using an image that tiles seamlessly is also a good idea so that your background appears to be one large image that covers the entire page. Fireworks includes a number of features that can help you create background images.

Are backgrounds always patterns?

Although many backgrounds repeat a pattern of some kind, a background image can also be an image that is big enough to fill the entire screen. Because a background image tiles, a vertical image creates a stripe across the top of the page, and a horizontal image creates a stripe along the left edge of the page.

Change the Background Color

You can add color to your Web pages by changing the background color. Dreamweaver offers a selection of Web-safe colors that are designed to display well on all computer monitors.

Change the Background Color

① Click **Page Properties** in the Property inspector.

The Page Properties dialog box appears.

② Click **Appearance**.

③ Click the **Background color** ☐ to open the color menu (◌ changes to ✐).

④ Click a color from the menu using the Eyedropper tool (✐).

⑤ Click **OK**.

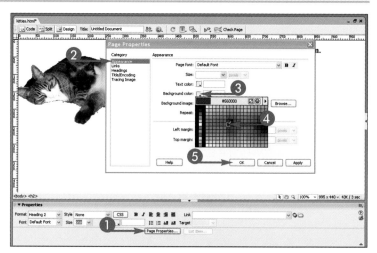

The background of your Web page displays in the color that you selected.

Note: *For additional information about Web color, see Chapter 5.*

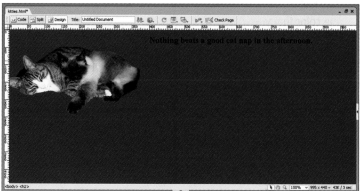

You can change the text color for the entire page using Dreamweaver's Page Properties.

When you alter page and text colors, make sure that the text is still readable. In general, light text colors work best against a dark background and dark text colors work best against a light background.

Change Text Colors

1 Click **Page Properties** in the Property inspector.

The Page Properties dialog box appears.

2 Click **Appearance**.

3 Click the **Text color** to open the color menu (changes to).

4 Click a color from the menu using the Eyedropper tool ().

5 Click **OK**.

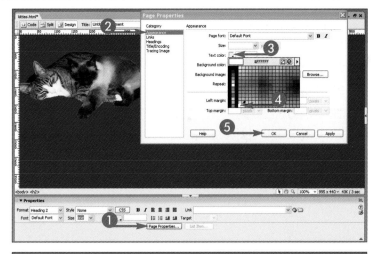

Any text on your Web page displays in the color that you selected.

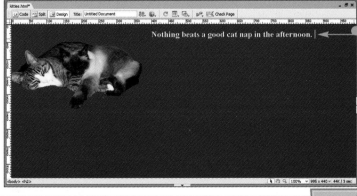

Insert a Flash File

You can add life to your Web page by adding Flash animations and slide shows. A Flash file is a multimedia file that is created with Adobe Flash or other software that supports the Flash format. Flash files are ideal for animated banners, cartoons, slide shows, interactive animations, and site navigation features.

Insert a Flash File

1 Position the mouse where you want to insert a Flash file.

2 Click **Insert**.

3 Click **Media**.

4 Click **Flash**.

The Select File dialog box appears.

5 Click here and select the folder that contains the Flash file.

Note: Flash filenames end with an `.swf` file extension.

6 Click the file that you want to insert into your Web page.

7 Click **OK**.

● The Flash icon appears in the Document window.

● You can change the size of the Flash movie by clicking and dragging its lower-left corner, or by entering a width and height in the Property inspector.

⑧ Click **Play** (▶ Play) in the Property inspector to test the Flash file.

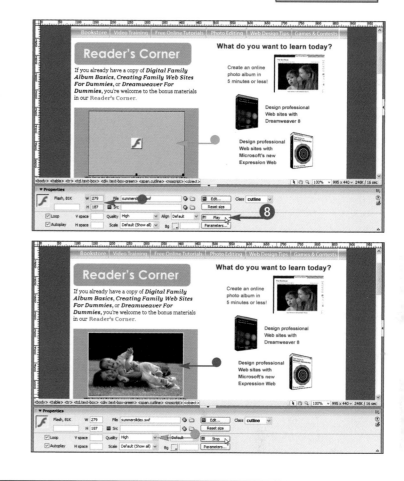

● The Flash file displays in your Dreamweaver document.

● You can click the **Quality** ⌄ and select the level of quality at which you want your movie to play. The higher the quality, the better it displays, but the longer it takes to download.

What are good uses for Flash on the Web?

Flash is an ideal tool for creating animations, interactive games, and other high-end features. You can even integrate video and audio files to create rich multimedia features for your Web site. You can learn more about Flash and see many examples at www.adobe.com.

You can save video and audio files in the Flash format and use Dreamweaver to add them to your Web pages.

Insert Flash Video Files

① Position the ▷ where you want to insert the Flash video file in the Document window.

② Click **Insert**.

③ Click **Media**.

④ Click **Flash Video**.

When you add Flash video files to a Web page, Web browsers are able to display them with a Flash player.

The Insert Flash Video dialog box appears.

⑤ Click **Browse** to select the Flash video file.

⑥ Click the **Detect Size** button to automatically enter the height and width.

⑦ Click **OK**.

The other settings are optional and can be left at the defaults.

● A Flash Video icon appears in the Document window.

⑧ You can change the Flash video settings in the Property inspector.

If the Flash plug-in is not installed on a user's Web browser, the browser asks whether the user wants to visit the site to download the plug-in.

⑨ Click 🔲 to test the Flash video file in a Web browser.

● The selected Web browser opens and displays the Web page.

Note: You must have the Flash 7 player, or a later version, on your computer to play a Flash video file.

TIP

What should I consider when adding multimedia content to my Web site?

Remember that although you may have the latest computer software and a fast connection, some of your visitors may not have the necessary multimedia players or bandwidth for your multimedia files. You can add Flash, video, sound, and other multimedia files to jazz up a Web site, but if your visitors do not have the right programs, then they cannot view them. Therefore it is very important to use compression and other techniques to keep file sizes small, and to offer links to players for any multimedia that you use.

Create a Rollover Image

Rollover images are designed to react when someone rolls a cursor over them. They are commonly used in navigation bars and other links, but they can also be used to add a little surprise to your pages. A rollover effect can be subtle or dramatic, depending on the differences between the two images that you use in the rollover, but both images must be the same size.

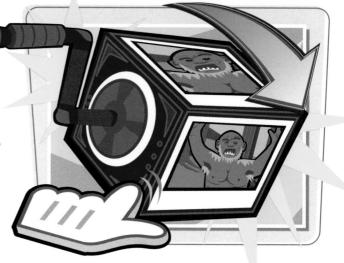

Create a Rollover Image

① Position the ⌖ where you want to insert the rollover image.

② Click **Insert**.

③ Click **Image Objects**.

④ Click **Rollover Image**.

The Insert Rollover Image dialog box appears.

⑤ Type an identifying name for scripting purposes.

⑥ Click **Browse** and select the first image.

⑦ Click **Browse** and select the second image.

⑧ Type a description of the images.

⑨ Type a URL if you want the rollover to serve as a link.

⑩ Click **OK**.

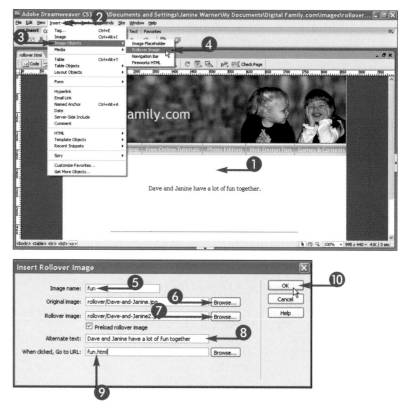

Dreamweaver automatically inserts the scripting that you need to make the rollover effect work.

● The first image in the rollover displays in the page.

⑪ Click  to view the page in a Web browser and test the rollover effect.

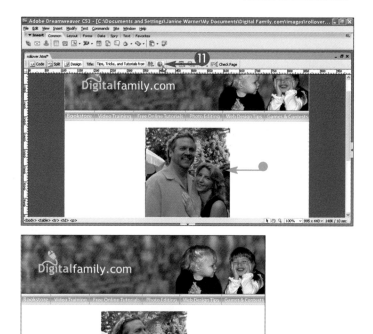

● When you roll your cursor over the first rollover image in a Web browser, the second image appears.

Dave and Janine have a lot of fun together.

TIP

How does the rollover image work?
The interactive effect of a rollover image requires more than HTML. Dreamweaver creates this effect by using a scripting language called JavaScript. JavaScript is used for many kinds of interactivity, from image swaps to pop-up windows. JavaScript is more complex than HTML code. Dreamweaver includes many other JavaScript features in the Behaviors panel. To see what other kinds of behaviors are available, use the Window menu to select Behaviors.

Insert a
Navigation Bar

You can increase the functionality of your Web site with a navigation bar. If your Web site consists of more than one page, then you can make it easier for your visitors to get around. A navigation bar is the best way to ensure that links to all of your main pages are available throughout your Web site.

Insert a Navigation Bar

① Position the ⌖ where you want to insert the navigation bar.

② Click **Insert**.

③ Click **Image Objects**.

④ Click **Navigation Bar**.

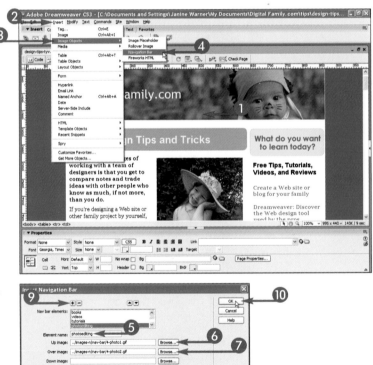

⑤ Type a name to identify the rollover in the script.

⑥ Click **Browse** and select the first Up image.

⑦ Click **Browse** and select the first Over image.

⑧ Click **Browse** and choose the page that the navigation button will link to.

⑨ Click the plus sign and repeat Steps **5** to **8** for each navigation rollover.

⑩ Click **OK**.

● Dreamweaver automatically inserts the scripting that is needed to make the rollover effects work.

The Up images display for each of the navigation buttons.

⓫ Click 🌐 to preview the page in a Web browser and test the rollover effects.

● When you roll your cursor over the navigation buttons in a Web browser, the rollover images display.

TIP

Where should I insert a navigation bar?

As a general rule, you want the navigation bar to be in the same place on every page. Most designers place them at the edge of a page where they cannot interfere with the design. It is common for Web pages to have left-hand navigation bars, or for navigation bars to be inserted across the top or bottom of a page. Right-hand navigation bars are also fine. Horizontal navigation bars are somewhat limited by the available space across the Web browser window, so some designers use them in combination with side navigation bars to highlight subsections of a Web site.

Creating Hyperlinks

Links, also called hyperlinks, are used to connect related information. Using Dreamweaver, you can create links from one page to another in your Web site, or to other Web sites on the Internet, and you can also create e-mail links and image maps. This chapter shows you how to create links using both text and images.

Link to Other Pages in Your Web Site

Dreamweaver makes it easy to create a link from one page in your Web site to another page so that your visitors can navigate your Web site.

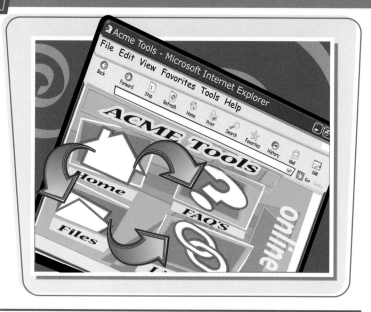

Link to Other Pages in Your Web Site

CREATE A LINK

① Click and drag to select the text that you want to turn into a link.

② Click the **Link** 📁 in the Property inspector.

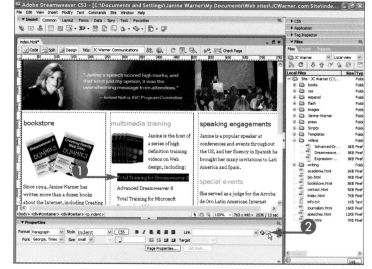

The Select File dialog box appears.

③ Click here and select the folder that contains the destination page.

④ Click the HTML file to which you want to link.

⑤ Click **OK**.

● The new link appears in color and underlined.

Note: Links are not clickable in the Document window.

● You can click 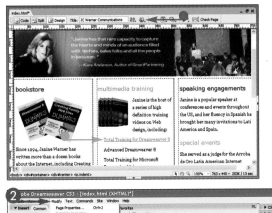 to test the link by previewing the file in a Web browser, such as Firefox or Internet Explorer.

OPEN AND EDIT A LINKED PAGE

① Click anywhere on the text of the link whose destination you want to open.

② Click **Modify**.

③ Click **Open Linked Page**.

The link destination opens in a Document window, allowing you to edit that document.

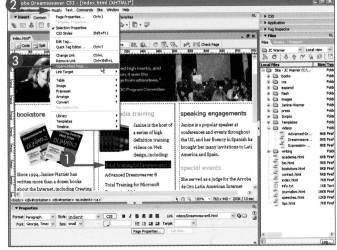

TIP

How should I organize the files that make up my Web site?

You should keep the files that make up your Web site in one main folder that you define as your local site root folder. This enables you to easily find pages and images, and create links between your pages. It also ensures that all of the links work correctly when you transfer the files to a Web server. If you have many pages under one section, you can create subfolders to further divide the file structure of your site. You may also want to create a separate folder for images. For more information on setting up your Web site, see Chapter 2. For more information on transferring files to a Web server, see Chapter 14.

Link to Another Web Site

You can link from your Web site to any other Web site on the Internet, giving your visitors access to additional information and providing valuable references to related information.

Link to Another Web Site

① Click and drag to select the text that you want to turn into a link.

② Type the Web address of the destination page in the Link field.

Note: you must type **http://** before the Web address.

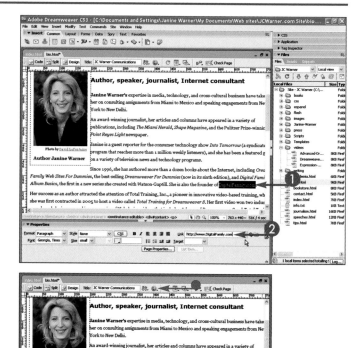

● The new link appears in color and underlined.

Note: Links are not clickable in the Document window.

● You can click 🌐 to test the link by previewing the file in a Web browser.

Note: To preview a Web page in a Web browser, see Chapter 2.

When you test the link in a Web browser while you are connected to the Internet, it opens the linked site, even if the page that contains the link is on your hard drive.

REMOVE A LINK

① Select the text of the link that you want to remove.

② Click **Modify**.

③ Click **Remove Link**.

Dreamweaver removes the link, and the text no longer appears in color and underlined.

TIP

How do I ensure that my links to other Web sites always work?

You do not have control over the Web pages on other Web sites to which you have linked. If you have linked to a Web page whose file is later renamed or taken offline, your viewers receive an error message when they click the link on your Web site. Maintain your Web site by periodically checking your links. You can also use software or Web site tune-up services, such as www.netmechanic.com, to perform this check for you. Although neither method can bring back a Web page that no longer exists, both methods combined can tell you which links you need to remove or update.

Use an Image as a Link

You can use an image to create a link to another page or Web site in much the same way that you create a link with text. Using images as links is a very common way to build a Web site's main navigation system, for example, using a row of images that link to all of the main pages of the Web site.

Use an Image as a Link

CREATE AN IMAGE LINK

① Click the image that you want to turn into a link.

② Click the **Link** 🗀.

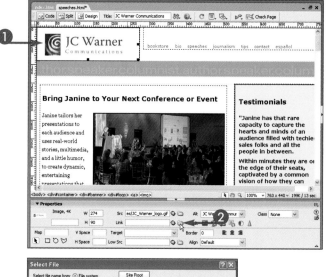

The Select File dialog box appears.

③ Click here and select the folder that contains the destination page.

④ Click the HTML file to which you want to link.

⑤ Click **OK**.

Your image becomes a link.

● Dreamweaver automatically inserts the filename and path to the linked page.

● You can click to test the link by previewing your page in a Web browser.

Note: To preview a page in a Web browser, see Chapter 2.

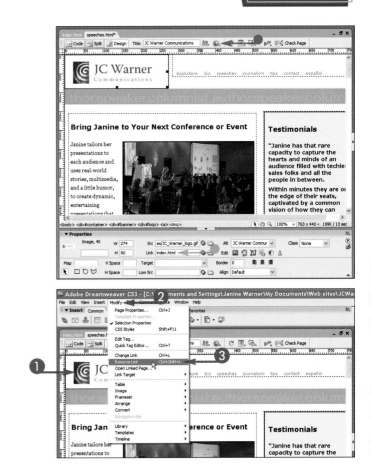

REMOVE A LINK FROM AN IMAGE

1. Click a linked image.

2. Click **Modify**.

3. Click **Remove Link**.

Dreamweaver removes the link.

 TIPS

How do I create a navigation bar for my Web page?

Many Web sites include sets of images that act as link buttons on the top, side, or bottom of each page. These button images allow viewers to navigate through the pages of the Web site. You can create these button images by using an image-editing program such as Adobe Photoshop or Adobe Fireworks, and then use Dreamweaver to insert them into the page and create the links.

How will visitors to my Web site know to click an image?

When a visitor rolls a cursor over an image that serves as a link, their cursor turns into a hand. You can make it clearer which images are linked by putting links in context with other content, and by grouping links to let visitors know that images are clickable.

Create a Jump Link within a Page

You can create a link to other content on the same page. Same-page links, often called jump links or anchor links, are commonly used on long pages when you want to provide an easy way to navigate to relevant information lower on the page.

You create a jump link by first placing a named anchor where you want the link to go to, and then linking from the text or image to the named anchor point.

① Position the ⦜ where you want to insert the named anchor.

② Click **Insert**.

③ Click **Named Anchor**.

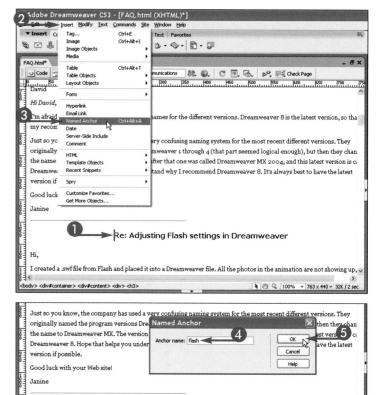

The Named Anchor dialog box appears.

④ Type a name for the anchor.

⑤ Click **OK**.

● An anchor appears in the Document window.

6 Click and drag to select the text that you want to link to the anchor.

7 Click 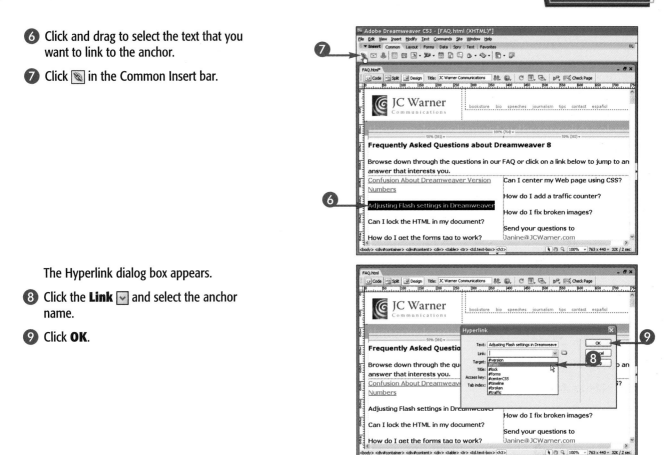 in the Common Insert bar.

The Hyperlink dialog box appears.

8 Click the **Link** ⬇ and select the anchor name.

9 Click **OK**.

TIP

Why would you create a jump link to something on the same page?

Web designers often use jump links, or same-page hyperlinks, to make it easier to find text that appears lower on a page. For example, these links are frequently used as Back to Top links that bring you to the beginning of a page when you click a link lower on the page. If you have a Web page that is a glossary, same-page links allow you to link to different parts of the glossary from a link menu at the top of the page. A Frequently Asked Questions (FAQ) page is another example of when to use same-page links, because you can list all of your questions at the top of the page to make it easier to find the answers.

Links do not have to lead just to other Web pages. You can also link to other file types, such as image files, word processing documents, PDF files, and multimedia files. Many of these files require their own players, but as long as your visitor has the required program, the file opens automatically when the user clicks the link.

Create a Link to Another File Type

① Click and drag to select the text that you want to turn into a link.

② Click the **Link** in the Property inspector.

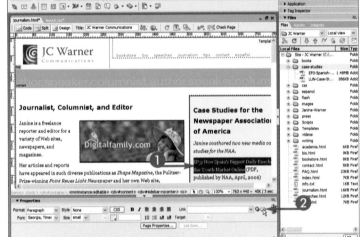

The Select File dialog box appears.

③ Click here and select the folder that contains the destination file.

④ Click the file to which you want to link.

⑤ Click **OK**.

● The new link appears in color and underlined.

Note: Links are not clickable in the Document window.

● You can click to preview the link in a Web browser.

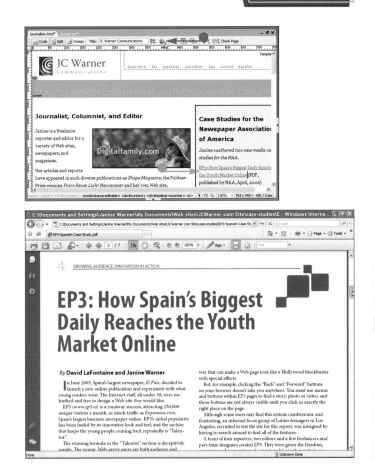

When you click the link in a Web browser, the linked file opens.

In this example, a PDF document opens in the Web browser window.

TIP

How do users see files that are not HTML documents?

What users see when they click links to other types of files depends on how they have configured their Web browser and what applications they have installed on their computer. For example, if you link to a QuickTime movie (which has a `.mov` file extension), your visitors need to have a player that can display QuickTime movies. It is always good practice to include a link to the player for any special file type, to make it easy for users to find and download it if they choose.

Create an Image Map

You can link different areas of an image to different pages with an image map. First, you define areas of the image, called *hotspots*, using Dreamweaver's image-mapping tools, and then you turn them into links.

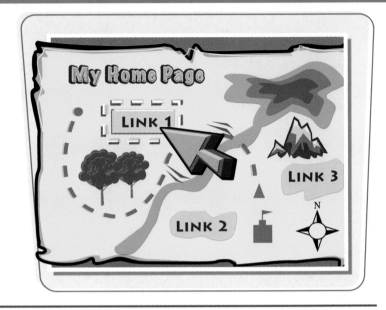

Create an Image Map

① Click an image.

② Type a name for the image map.

Note: You cannot use spaces or special characters in an image map name.

③ Click a drawing tool.

   You can create rectangular shapes with the Rectangular Hotspot tool (▭), oval shapes with the Oval Hotspot tool (◯), and irregular shapes with the Polygon Hotspot tool (♡).

④ Draw an area on the image using the tool that you selected.

● If a message appears instructing you to describe the image map in the "alt" file, click **OK** to close the dialog box and type a description in the Alt field.

   To delete a hotspot, you can select it, and then press Delete.

⑤ Click ▭.

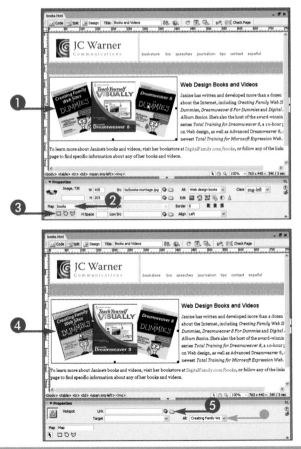

The Select File dialog box appears.

6 Click here and select the folder that contains the destination file.

7 Click the file to which you want to link.

8 Click **OK**.

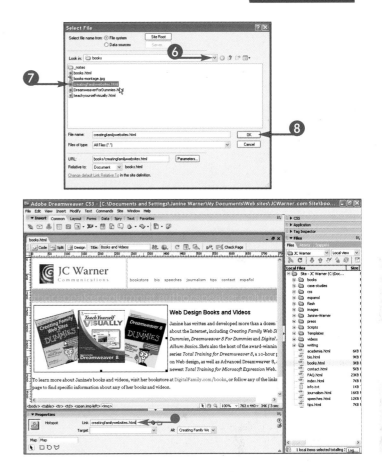

● The area defined by the selected shape is linked to the selected file, and the name and path to the file display in the Property inspector.

In this example, the image of the book, *Creating Family Web Sites for Dummies*, links to a page about the book.

You can repeat Steps **3** to **8** to add other linked areas to your image.

The image-map shapes do not appear when you open the page in a Web browser.

TIP

Can image maps be used for geographical maps that link to multiple locations?

Yes. An interactive geographical map, such as a map of Latin America, is a common place to see hotspots in action. You can create one by adding a graphic image of a map to your Web page and then defining a hotspot over each location to which you want to link. Use the Polygon tool (▱) to draw around boundaries that do not follow a square shape. Finally, assign a different link to each hotspot.

Create a Link Using the Files Panel

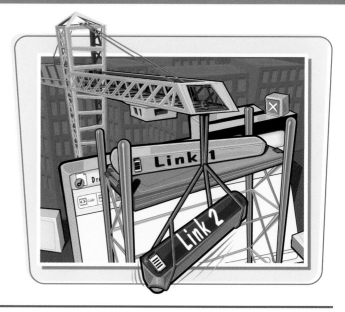

Dreamweaver provides multiple options for creating links. For example, you can create links quickly and easily using either the Property inspector or the Files panel.

Your Web pages only display in the Files panel if you have set up your Web site in Dreamweaver, an important first step that is covered in Chapter 2.

Create a Link Using the Files Panel

Note: *Arrange your workspace so that both the Document window and the Files panel are visible for this task. You can open the Files panel by clicking* **Window** *and then clicking* **Files**.

1 Click and drag to select the text that you want to turn into a link.

2 Click **Point to File** (⬚).

3 Drag the cursor until it is over the file that you want to link to in the Files panel.

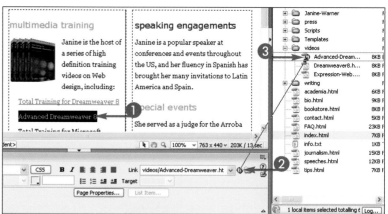

● The new link appears in color and underlined.

● The destination file displays in the Link field in the Property inspector.

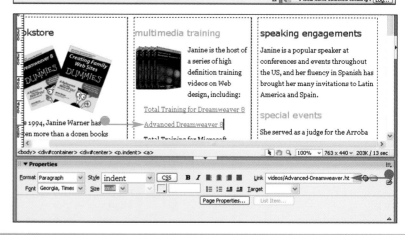

You can create a link that, when clicked, opens a new Web browser window to display the destination page.

Opening a new browser window allows a user to keep the previous Web page open.

Open a Linked Page in a New Browser Window

① Click and drag to select the link that you want to open in a new browser window.

② Click the **Target** ⊡.

③ Click **_blank**.

④ Click ⊡ to preview the page in a Web browser.

⑤ Click the link.

The link destination appears in a new browser window, and the page with the link remains open behind the linked page.

Note: If the user's browser window is set to fill the entire page, the original Web page will not be visible when the linked page is opened.

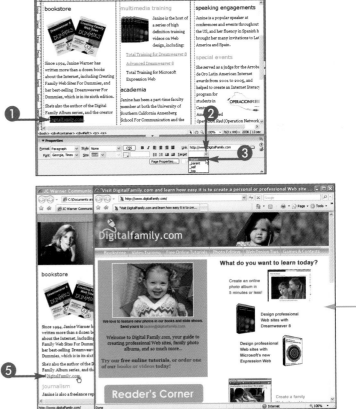

Create an E-Mail Link

You can create an e-mail link in your Web page. When a user clicks the link, it launches an e-mail program on the user's computer, creates a message, and inserts the e-mail address into the Address field.

Create an E-Mail Link

1. Click to select the text or image that you want to turn into an e-mail link.

2. Click the **Email Link** button (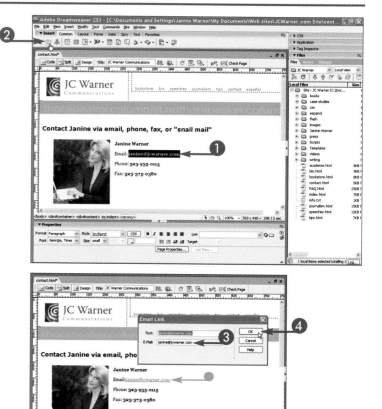).

Note: If the email link button is not visible, click the Common tab in the Insert bar.

The Email Link dialog box appears, with the selected text in the Text field.

3. Type the e-mail address to which you want to link.

4. Click **OK**.

Dreamweaver creates your e-mail link, and the selected text displays in color and underlined.

To test the link, you can click to preview the page in a Web browser.

Note: For an e-mail link to work properly, a user must have an e-mail program installed on their computer.

You can automatically verify the links on a Web page. Using Dreamweaver's link-testing features, you can also receive a report that lists any links that are broken.

There are many ways in which links can become broken. Dreamweaver makes it easy to find and fix them.

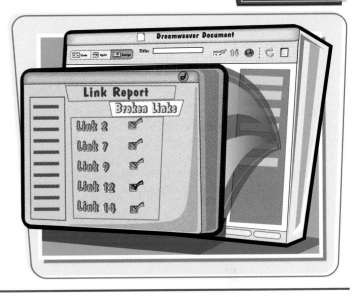

Check Links

1. Click **File**.
2. Click **Check Page**.
3. Click **Links**.

- Dreamweaver checks the local links and lists any broken links that it finds in the Results panel.

Note: *Dreamweaver cannot verify links to Web pages on external sites.*

- You can edit a broken destination or image file by selecting the name of the link in the Results panel, and then clicking the **Browse** 🔲 to locate the correct file.

Change the Color of Links on a Page

You can change the color of the links on your Web page to make them match the visual style of the other text and images on your page. You can also remove the underline under linked text.

① Click **Modify**.

② Click **Page Properties**.

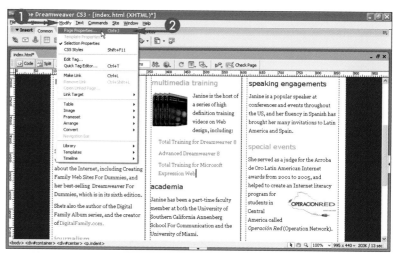

The Page Properties dialog box appears.

③ Click **Links**.

④ Click the **Link Color** ☐ (⟨ changes to ⟩).

⑤ Click a color using the ⟩ tool.

⑥ Repeat Steps **4** and **5** to specify colors for Visited, Rollover, and Active links.

● You can click the **Color Picker** (◉) to select a custom color.

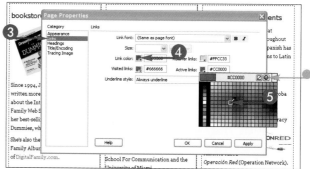

⑦ Click the **Underline Style** ☑.

⑧ Click **Never Underline** to remove the underline from all of your links.

⑨ Click **OK**.

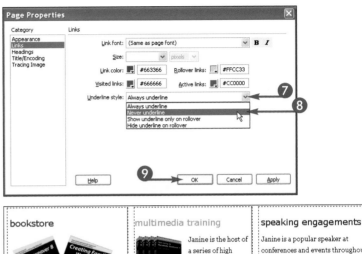

● The links display without underlines in the specified Link color.

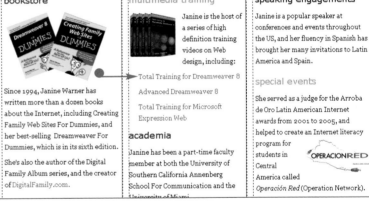

bookstore

Since 1994, Janine Warner has written more than a dozen books about the Internet, including Creating Family Web Sites For Dummies, and her best-selling Dreamweaver For Dummies, which is in its sixth edition.

She's also the author of the Digital Family Album series, and the creator of DigitalFamily.com.

multimedia training

Janine is the host of a series of high definition training videos on Web design, including:

Total Training for Dreamweaver 8

Advanced Dreamweaver 8

Total Training for Microsoft Expression Web

academia

Janine has been a part-time faculty member at both the University of Southern California Annenberg School For Communication and the University of Miami

speaking engagements

Janine is a popular speaker at conferences and events throughout the US, and her fluency in Spanish has brought her many invitations to Latin America and Spain.

special events

She served as a judge for the Arroba de Oro Latin American Internet awards from 2001 to 2005, and helped to create an Internet literacy program for students in Central America called *Operación Red* (Operation Network).

TIPS

What color will my links be if I do not choose colors for them?

Blue is the default link color in the Dreamweaver Document window. What viewers see when the page opens in a Web browser depends on their browser settings. By default, most Web browsers display unvisited links as blue, visited links as purple, and rollover links as red.

How can I override the link colors that I set?

Sometimes you may need to change the color of a linked word to something other than the set link color of a page—for example, if it is set against a different background color or you want it to stand out better. Select the text and use the Font field in the Property inspector to select a color. Once you change it, the text always appears in that color, even after it is visited.

Editing Table Designs in a Web Page

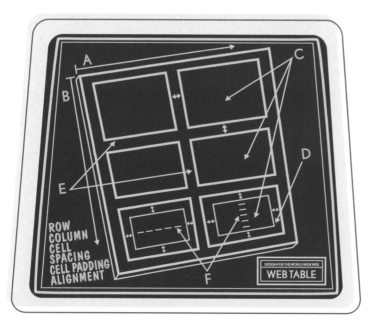

Tables are an ideal way to format tabular data, such as the information that you find in a spreadsheet. You can also use tables to create complex designs, even within the constraints of HTML. This chapter shows you how to create and format tables.

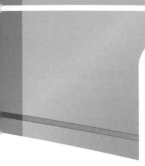

Insert a Table into a Web Page

You can use tables to organize and design pages that contain financial data, text, images, and multimedia. Dreamweaver's layout features enable you to create simple tables for tabular data, or complex tables for sophisticated layouts and designs. You can also insert tables between existing elements on a page.

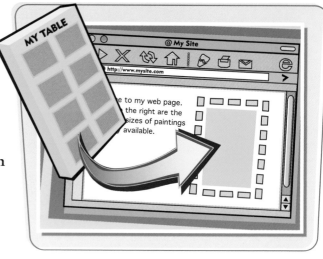

Insert a Table into a Web Page

INSERT A TABLE

① Position where you want to insert a table.

By default, the cursor snaps to the left margin, although you can change the table alignment.

② Click **Insert**.

③ Click **Table**.

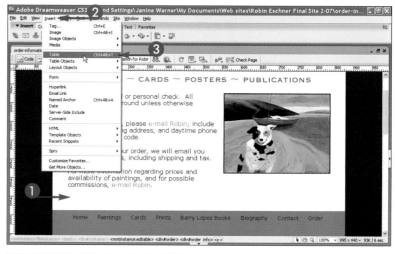

The Table dialog box appears.

④ Type the number of rows and columns that you want in your table.

⑤ Type the width of your table.

You can set the width in pixels, or as a percentage of the page, by clicking and selecting your choice of measurements.

⑥ Click to select a Table Header option.

⑦ Click **OK**.

● An empty table appears, aligned to the left by default.

● You can click ⏷ and select a different alignment.

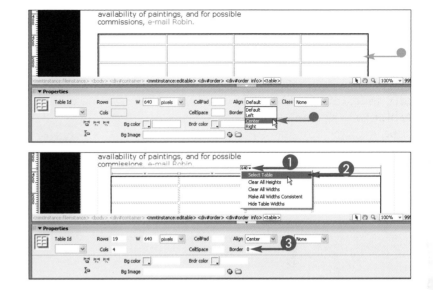

TURN OFF TABLE BORDERS

① Click ⏷.

② Click **Select Table**.

③ Type the number **0** in the Border field.

④ Press `Enter` (`Return`).

When you view the page in a Web browser, the dashed table border disappears.

TIPS

How do I change the appearance of the content inside my table?

You can specify the size, style, and color of text inside a table in the same way that you format text on a Web page. Similarly, you can control the appearance of an image inside a table in the same way that you can control it outside a table. For more information on formatting text, see Chapter 5; for more information on images, see Chapter 6.

Why would I turn off table borders?

Table borders can help to define the edges of a table and to organize columnar data, such as a financial report. However, if you want to use a table to arrange photos and text within the design of your page, then you can have a cleaner layout if you set the border to zero so that it becomes invisible. You can set the table border to 1 pixel for a slim border, or try 5 or 10 pixels if you want a thick border.

Insert Content into a Table

You can fill the cells of your table with text, images, multimedia files, form elements, and even other tables, just as you would add any them anywhere else on a page.

Insert Content into a Table

INSERT TEXT

1 Click to place your cursor inside the table cell.

2 Type text into the cell.

Note: *To format your text, see Chapter 5.*

INSERT AN IMAGE

1 Click inside a table cell.

2 Click the **Image** button ().

The Select Image Source dialog box appears.

3 Click here and select the folder that contains your image.

4 Click an image file.

5 Click **OK**.

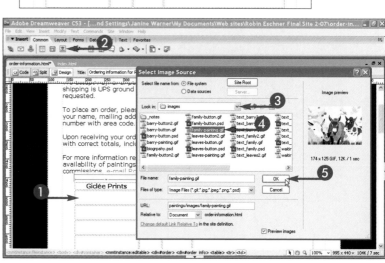

- The image appears in the table cell.

- If the image is larger than the cell, the cell expands to accommodate the image.

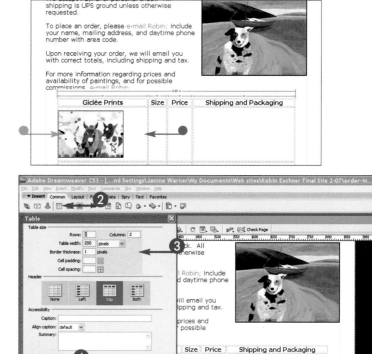

INSERT A TABLE WITHIN A TABLE

1 Click inside a table cell.

2 Click the **Table** button (▦).

The Table dialog box appears.

3 Type values in the fields to define the characteristics of the table.

4 Click **OK**.

- The new table appears within the table cell.

TIP

How can I add captions to images on my Web page?

The best way to add a caption to the top, bottom, or side of an image is by creating a two-celled table. Place the image in one cell and the caption in the other. You can then adjust the size and alignment of the table to position the captioned image within the rest of the content on your Web page.

You can change the background of a table, or only change the background of a cell, a row, or a column. This is a great way to add a design element or to call attention to a section of a table. Just like the background of a Web page, you can change the background color of a table, or fill the background of a table with an image. For more information on Web page backgrounds, see Chapter 6.

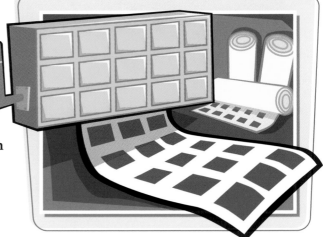

Change the Background of a Table

CHANGE THE BACKGROUND COLOR

1. Click to select a table or individual cell, or click and drag to select a row or column of cells.

2. Click the **Background** 🔲 to open the color menu (🔍 changes to ✏️).

3. Click a color anywhere on the screen.

● You can click the **Color Picker** button (🔲) to select a custom color.

● Click the **Default Color** button (🔲) to remove a specified color.

● The color fills the background of the selected cells.

● You can also type a color name or hexadecimal color code into the Color field.

Note: To change the font color on a Web page, see Chapter 5.

ADD A BACKGROUND IMAGE TO A TABLE

1 Click a corner to select a table or cell, or click and drag to select multiple cells.

2 Click the **Background Image** 📁 in the Property inspector.

The Select Image Source dialog box appears.

3 Click ▾ and select the folder that contains your image.

4 Click an image file.

5 Click **OK**.

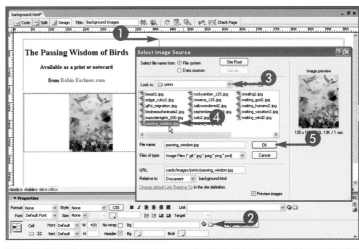

The table or cell background fills with the image.

If the cell space is greater than the image size, the image tiles fill the available area. If the image is larger than the cell, any part of the image that extends beyond the boundaries of the cell will not be visible.

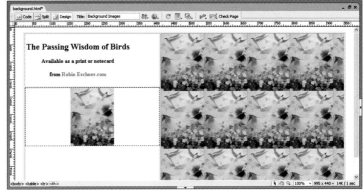

 TIP

How can I change the background of a table cell?

Click inside a cell and then specify the background color using the Background Color 🔲 in the Property inspector, or insert a background image by clicking and selecting an image from the Select Image Source dialog box. You can give each cell a different background or use one color to create an appearance of a solid area. You can also fill a cell with one large image in the background. You can then add text and other elements over the background.

Change the Cell Padding in a Table

You can change the cell padding to add space between a table's content and its borders.

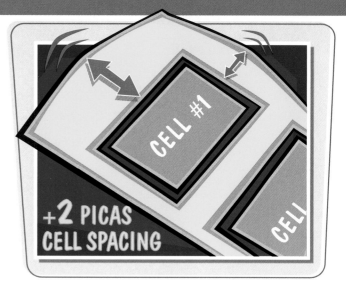

+2 PICAS
CELL SPACING

Change the Cell Padding in a Table

1 Click the top-left corner of the table to select it.

2 In the **CellPad** field in the Property inspector, type the amount of padding in pixels.

3 Press Enter (Return).

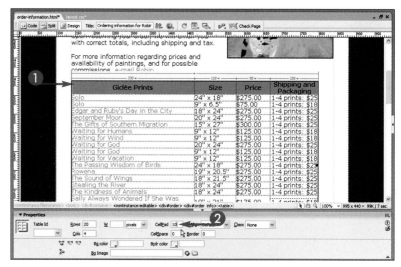

● The space changes between the table content and the table borders.

Note: Adjusting the cell padding affects all of the cells in a table. You cannot adjust the padding of individual cells by using the CellPad field.

You can change cell spacing to adjust the distance that cells are from each other.

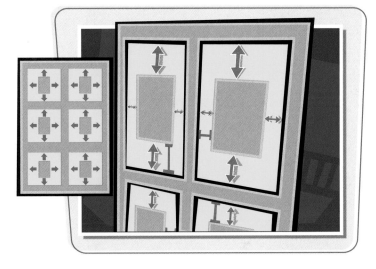

Change the Cell Spacing in a Table

1 Click the top-left corner of the table to select it.

2 In the **CellSpace** field, type the amount of spacing in pixels.

3 Press Enter (Return).

The cell spacing changes.

● You can change the width of the table or a column by clicking and dragging the cell borders.

Note: *Adjusting the cell spacing affects all of the cell borders in the table. You cannot adjust the spacing of individual cell borders by using the CellSpace field.*

Change the Alignment of a Table

You can change the alignment of a table and wrap text and other content around it, much like you would do with images and other elements.

Change the Alignment of a Table

1 Click the top-left corner of the table to select it.

2 Click the **Align** ☑.

3 Click an alignment option.

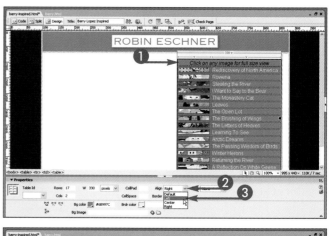

The table aligns in the page.

You can align the content in your table cells horizontally and vertically. For example, you can center elements or move them to the top or bottom of a cell.

Change the Alignment of Cell Content

1 Click and drag to select an entire column or row.

You can Shift-click, or click and drag, to select multiple cells.

2 Click the **Horizontal** ☑.

3 Click a horizontal alignment.

To change the vertical alignment, repeat Steps **1** to **3** and select a vertical alignment option.

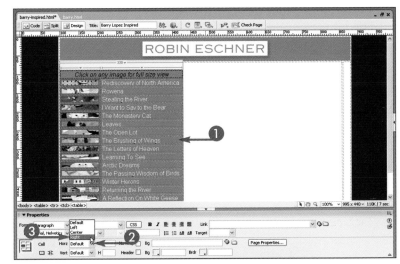

● The content aligns within the cell.

In this example, horizontal alignment is used to align the text in these cells to the right.

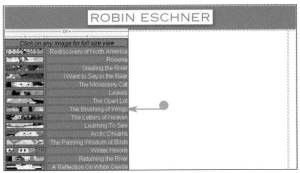

Insert or Delete a Row or Column

You can insert cells into your table to add content or to create space between elements. You can also delete rows or columns to remove them when they are not needed.

Insert or Delete a Row or Column

INSERT A ROW OR COLUMN

1 Click the top-left corner of the table to select it.

2 Type the number of rows and columns that you want in the Property inspector.

3 Press **Enter** (**Return**).

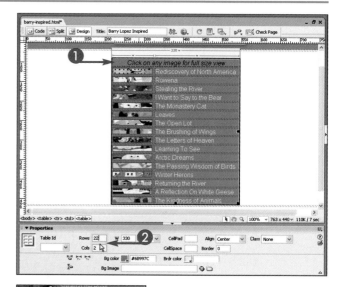

● Empty rows or columns appear in the table.

To add a row or column in the middle of a table, you can right-click inside an existing cell, click **Table**, and then click **Insert Row** or **Insert Column** from the menu that appears.

You can also click **Modify**, click **Table**, and then click **Insert Row** or **Insert Column**.

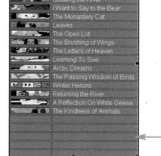

DELETE A ROW OR COLUMN

1 Select the cells that you want to delete by **Shift**-clicking, or clicking and dragging over them.

2 Press **Delete**.

Beast	12.5"x16.5"	$150.00	1-4 prints: $18
Rocky and Amber's Very Fine Day on the Cascapedia	23" x 19"	$275.00	1-4 prints: $25

Home   Paintings   Cards   Prints   Barry Lopez Books   Biography   Contact   Order

1

● The selected table cells disappear.

Note: *The content of a cell is deleted when you delete the cell.*

You can also delete cells by right-clicking inside the cells, clicking **Table**, and then clicking either **Delete Row** or **Delete Column** from the menu that appears.

You can also click **Modify**, click **Table**, and then click either **Delete Row** or **Delete Column**.

The Kindness of Animals	18" x 24"	$275.00	1-4 prints: $25
Sally Always Wondered If She Was Adopted	10" x 21"	$175.00	1-4 prints: $18
Mazzoleni's Girls	19" x 34"	$275.00	1-4 prints: $25
Beast	12.5"x16.5"	$150.00	1-4 prints: $18
Rocky and Amber's Very Fine Day on the Cascapedia	23" x 19"	$275.00	1-4 prints: $25

Home   Paintings   Cards   Prints   Barry Lopez Books   Biography   Contact   Order

TIPS

Does Dreamweaver warn me if a deleted cell contains content?

Dreamweaver does not warn you if the cells that you are deleting in a table contain content. This is because Dreamweaver assumes that you also want to delete the cell content. If you accidentally remove content when deleting rows or columns, you can click **Edit** and then click **Undo** to undo your last action.

How do I move content around a table?

You can move the contents of a table cell by clicking to select any image, text, or element in the cell and then dragging it out of the table or into another cell. You can also use the Copy and Paste commands to move content from one cell to another, or to another part of a page.

Split or Merge Table Cells

You can create more elaborate page designs by splitting or merging cells in a table to create larger cells adjacent to smaller ones. You can then insert text, images, and other content into the cells.

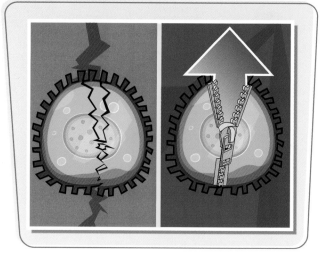

Split or Merge Table Cells

SPLIT A TABLE CELL

① Click to place your cursor in the cell that you want to split.

② Click **Modify**.

③ Click **Table**.

④ Click **Split Cell**.

● You can also split a cell by clicking the **Split Cell** button (⌗) in the Property inspector.

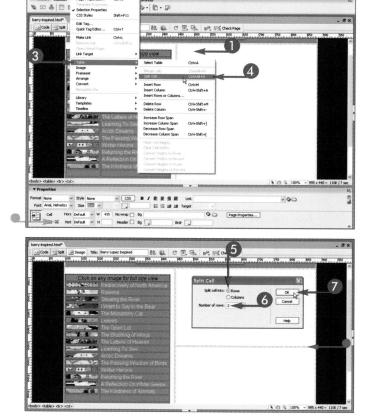

The Split Cell dialog box appears.

⑤ Click **Rows** or **Columns** to split the cell (○ changes to ◉).

⑥ Type the number of rows or columns.

⑦ Click **OK**.

● The table cell splits.

MERGE TABLE CELLS

1 Click and drag to select the cells that you want to merge.

2 Click the **Merge** button (⊞) in the Property inspector.

You can also merge cells by clicking **Modify**, clicking **Table**, and then clicking **Merge Cells**.

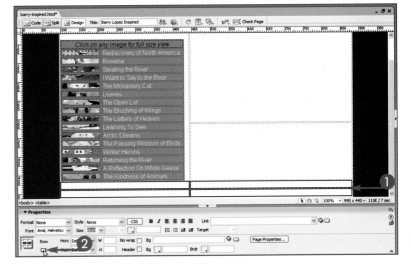

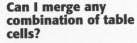

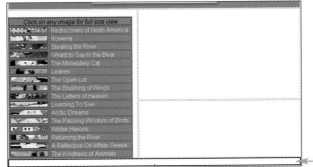

● The table cells merge.

Can I merge any combination of table cells?

No. The cells must have a rectangular arrangement. For example, you can merge all of the cells in a two-row-by-two-column table. However, you cannot select three cells that form an L shape and merge them into one cell.

Can I add as many cells as I want?

Yes, just make sure that your final table design displays well on a computer monitor. For example, although it is common to design Web pages that are long and require visitors to scroll down, it can be confusing to create overly wide pages that require scrolling right or left. Keep your overall page width under 780 pixels wide if you want it to display well on an 800-by-600 resolution computer monitor.

Change the Dimensions of a Cell

You can change the dimensions of individual table cells to better accommodate their content. As you enlarge and reduce cells, you can create more complex tables for more precise design control.

Change the Dimensions of a Cell

① Click to select the edge of a cell, and drag to adjust the size.

You can also click to place your cursor inside any cell and then enter a size in the Property inspector.

You can also specify a percentage of the table size instead of specifying pixels. For example, you can type **25** and select **percent** in the width box.

② Press Enter (Return).

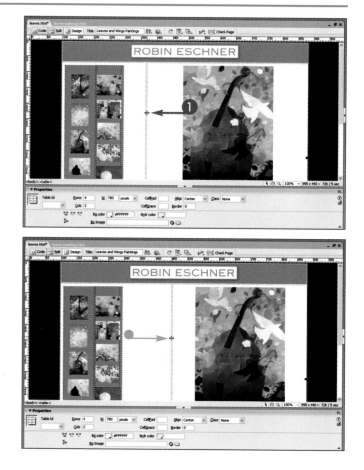

● The cell and its contents readjust to its new dimensions.

Note: *Cell dimensions may be constrained by content. For example, Dreamweaver cannot shrink a cell smaller than the size of the content that it contains.*

You can change the dimensions of your entire table. This helps to ensure that your content fits well within your Web page.

Change the Dimensions of a Table

1 Click the top-left corner of the table to select it.

2 Type a width.

3 Click here and select the width setting in pixels, or a percentage of the screen.

4 Press Enter (Return).

● The table readjusts to its new dimensions.

Note: *Table dimensions may be constrained by content. For example, Dreamweaver cannot shrink a table smaller than the size of the content that it contains.*

If you do not specify a height or width, the table automatically adjusts to fit the space that is available on the user's screen.

Use Percentages for Table Width

You can specify the size of a table using percentage instead of pixels. As a result, the table automatically adjusts to fit a user's browser window size.

When you define a table size as a percentage, it adjusts to fill that percentage of a user's browser window.

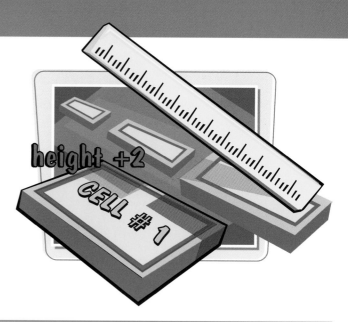

Use Percentages for Table Width

SET TABLE WIDTH AS A PERCENTAGE

1 Position the ꕯ where you want to insert a table.

By default, the cursor snaps to the left margin, although you can change the table alignment.

Note: *For instructions on creating a table, see the section "Insert a Table into a Web Page."*

2 Click **Insert**.

3 Click **Table**.

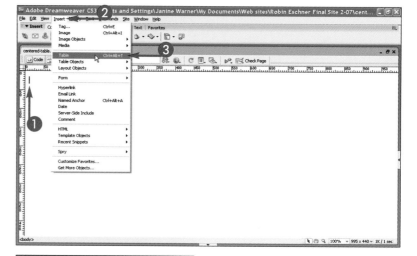

The Table dialog box appears.

4 Type the number of rows and columns that you want in your table.

5 Type the width of your table.

6 Click ꕯ and select **percent**.

7 Click **OK**.

An empty table appears (aligned to the left by default) and fills the available window, based on the percentage width that you specified.

● You can click here and enter a different percentage.

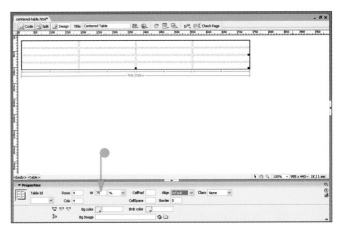

CENTER A TABLE

① Click the top-left corner of the table to select it.

② Click the **Align** ⬇.

③ Click **Center**.

● The table aligns in the center of the page.

 TIPS

What is a spacer image?

A spacer image is a transparent GIF image file that is used as a filler to invisibly control spacing on a Web page. Essentially, you insert a spacer image into a table cell and then use the height and width attributes to control the size of the image. The invisible spacer image ensures that blank spaces on your page remain consistent. This is important because Web browsers sometimes display elements closer together if there is no text or image to maintain consistent spacing within the design.

How do you make a spacer image?

You can create your own spacer image in an image-editing program, such as Adobe Photoshop or Fireworks. Create a new image and set the background color to transparent. Save it as a GIF file in your Web site folder. An ideal size for a spacer image is 10 pixels by 10 pixels; however, it can be any size. You can resize it in Dreamweaver to fit the space that you want to fill.

Creating Pages with Frames

You can divide the display area of a Web browser into multiple panes by creating frames. Frames offer another way to organize information by splitting up your pages. For example, you can keep linked content visible in one frame and target it to open in a different frame within the same browser window.

Introduction to Frames

Frames enable you to divide your Web page into multiple sections and display different content in each frame.

A common use of frames is to place a list of navigation links in one frame, and have the links open their destination pages in a larger content frame.

Set Up a Frame

You can create a framed Web site in Dreamweaver by dividing the Document window horizontally or vertically one or more times. Each frame is composed of a different Web page that you can link independently. All pages in a frameset are identified in a frameset page, and you must save them separately.

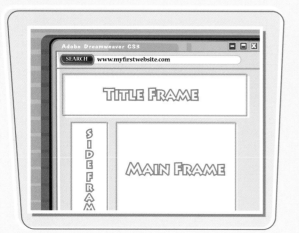

How Frames Work

Frames on a page operate independently of one another. As you scroll through the content of one frame, the content of the other frames remains fixed. You can create a link in one frame and target the link to open in any other frame.

Saving your frameset requires you to save each of the individual pages that appear in the frames, as well as the frameset that defines how each frame appears.

You first need to save all of the individual documents before you can preview your work in a Web browser or upload the frameset files to your Web site.

Save a Frameset

1 Click **File**.

2 Click **Save All**.

The Save Frameset command appears gray if the current frameset is already saved.

The Save As dialog box appears.

3 Click here and select the folder where you want to save the framed page.

4 Type a name for the first page in the frameset.

5 Click **Save**.

Repeat steps **3** through **5** for each file in the frameset.

Dreamweaver saves all of the files in the frameset.

Insert a Predefined Frameset

You can easily create popular frame styles using the predefined framesets. You can access frame styles from the Frames tab in the Insert panel. They are also available from the Sample Framesets that are featured in the new opening screen in Dreamweaver, and in the New Document window.

Insert a Predefined Frameset

① Click **File**.

② Click **New**.

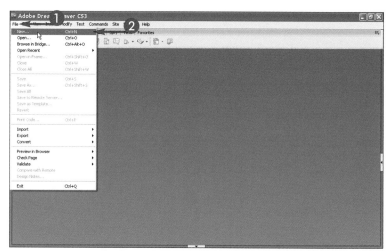

The New Document dialog box appears.

③ Click **Page from Sample**.

④ Click the **Frameset** 🗀.

⑤ Click a frameset design.

⑥ Click **Create**.

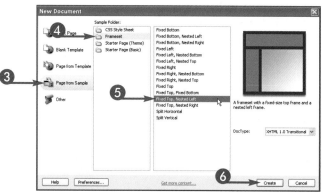

The Frame Tag Accessibility Attributes dialog box opens.

● You can turn disability features off in Dreamweaver's preferences by clicking this link.

⑦ Type a name and title for the frame, or accept the frame name that Dreamweaver automatically assigns.

⑧ Click **OK**.

Repeat steps **1** through **8** for each frame.

Dreamweaver automatically creates all of the frames in the work area and assigns each frame a name.

● The frameset properties appear in the Property inspector.

⑨ Click **Window**.

⑩ Click **Frames**.

● The Frames panel opens to display the frame names.

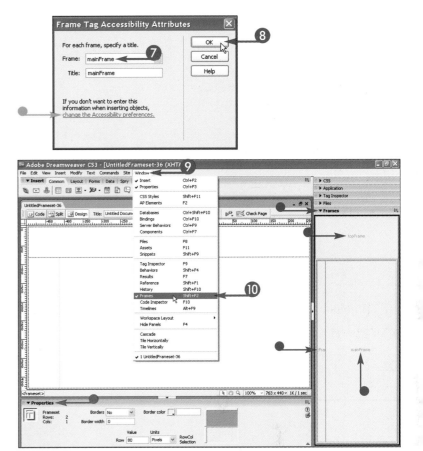

Can I save individual pages in my frameset separately?

Yes. You can save any of the pages within a frameset individually. Simply click to place your cursor in the frame area that you want to save, click **File**, and then click **Save**. Dreamweaver saves only the framed page that you have selected.

What steps do I take if I want to change just one frame?

You can open any existing page into a frame area. Place your mouse in the frame that you want to change, click **File**, and then click **Open** to open an existing page. You can also click **File** and then click **New** to create a new page in the designated frame area.

Divide a Page into Frames

You can split a Document window vertically to create a frameset with left and right frames, or you can split it horizontally to create a frameset with top and bottom frames. You can also combine them to create more complex frames, or add frames to a predefined frameset.

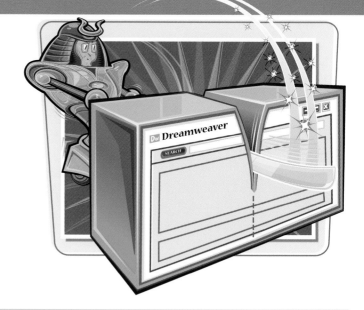

① Click **Modify**.

② Click **Frameset**.

③ Click a Split Frame command.

● The window splits into two frames. If content existed in the original page, then it shifts to one of the new frames.

● Scroll bars appear if the content extends outside the frame borders.

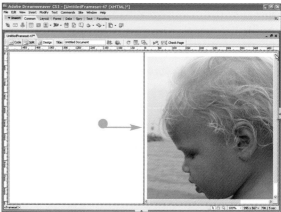

Create a Nested Frame

You can subdivide a frame of an existing frameset to create nested frames. With nested frames, you can organize the information in your site in a more complex way.

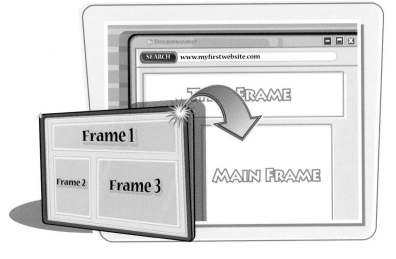

Create a Nested Frame

1 Click inside the frame that you want to subdivide.

2 Click **Modify**.

3 Click **Frameset**.

4 Click a Split Frame command.

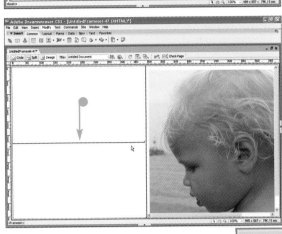

● Dreamweaver splits the selected frame into two frames, creating a nested frame.

You can continue to split your frames into more frames.

Change the Attributes of a Frame

You can change the dimensions of a frame to display the information more attractively inside it. You can also change scrolling and other options in the Property inspector.

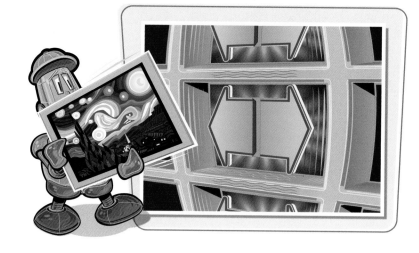

SPECIFY A COLUMN SIZE

1. Click a frame border to select the frame that you want to change.

2. Type a column size.

3. Click here and select the units that you want to use for the column size.

   You can select pixels, or a percentage for the display area.

4. Press **Enter** (**Return**).

● The column adjusts to the specified width.

● You can also click a frame border and drag it to the desired column width (⟨ changes to ↖↘).

SET FRAME ATTRIBUTES

1 Click **Window**.

2 Click **Frames**.

The Frames Advanced Layout panel opens.

3 In the Frames panel, click a frame to select it.

4 Click the Scroll .

5 Click a Scroll attribute.

You can also adjust other attributes for borders and scrolling in the Property inspector.

The frame scroll bar changes, based on the option you selected.

TIPS

Is there a shortcut for changing the dimensions of frames?

Yes. You can click and drag a frame border to quickly adjust the dimensions of a frame. The values in the Property inspector change as you drag the frame border.

Why would I want to change scrolling options?

When the content in a frame exceeds the dimensions of a Web browser window, you should include a scroll bar so that visitors can view all of your content. If you set the Scroll attribute to Yes in the Property inspector, then the scroll bar is always visible. If you set it to Auto, then a scroll bar appears only when needed.

Add Content to a Frame

You can insert text, images, and other content into a frame just as you would in an unframed page. You can also link existing pages into a frameset.

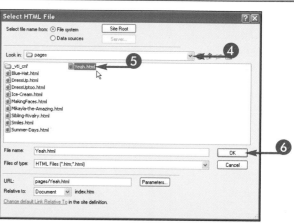

OPEN AN EXISTING FRAMESET

1 Click to position ▷ in the frame where you want to open an existing document.

2 Click **File**.

3 Click **Open in Frame**.

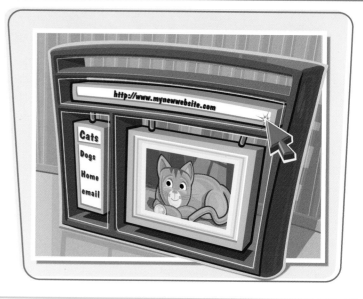

The Select HTML File dialog box appears.

4 Click here and select a folder.

5 Click the file that you want to open in the frame.

6 Click **OK**.

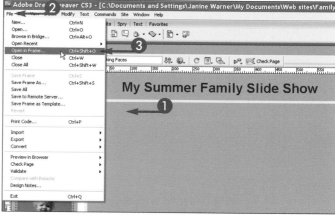

● The selected page appears in the frame area.

● If the content extends beyond the frame, then scroll bars automatically appear.

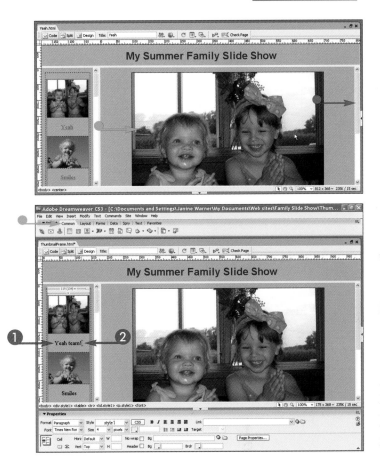

ADD NEW CONTENT TO A FRAME

① Click inside the frame where you want to add text.

② Type the text that you want to display.

● You can also add images, tables, or other elements by clicking the **Common** tab and then clicking the **Insert Image** button (▣) or the **Insert Table** button (▦) from the Insert panel.

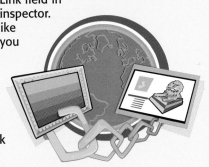

TIPS

Can I link a frame to a page on the Web?

Yes. You can link to an external Web page address by using the Link field in the Property inspector. However, unlike other pages, you must specify the target. To create targeted links, see the task, "Create a Link to a Frame."

Can I add as much content as I want to a frame page?

Yes. A frame page is just like any other page. You can add as much text, and as many images, as you want. However, if you have a small frame, then you can have better design results by limiting the text within that frame page to fit the small space.

You can delete existing frames or create new frames in a frameset to change or expand a design.

① Position the mouse on the border of the frame that you want to delete (◊ changes to ↘).

② Click and drag the border to the edge of the window.

Dreamweaver deletes the frame.

Before you can target links in one frame to open in another frame, you need to ensure that all of your frames have names. You use frame names to identify where the linked page should open in the frameset. Frame names are visible in the Frames panel.

This is Fred and Sarah, two good frames of mine.

Fred

Sarah

Frame 1

Frame 2

Name a Frame

If the Frames panel is not open, you can click **Window** and then click **Frames** to display it.

① Click to select the frame that you want to name in the Frames panel.

② Type a name for the frame.

③ Press Enter (Return).

● The new name of the frame appears in the Frames panel and in the Property inspector.

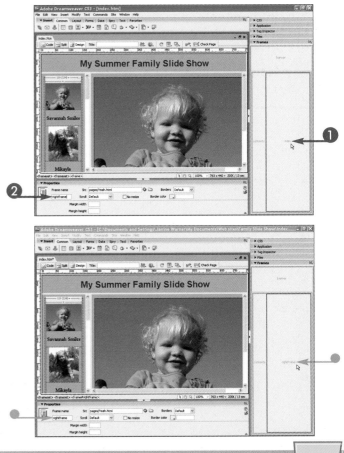

You can create links in one frame that open a page in another frame. This is a common technique for navigation rows and other links that you want to continue to display when the linked page opens. For more information about creating links, see Chapter 7.

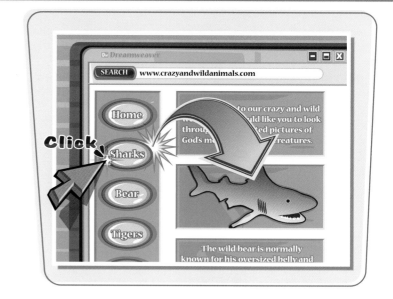

Create a Link to a Frame

① Click to select the text or image that you want to turn into a link.

② Click 🗀 in the Property inspector.

The Select File dialog box opens.

③ Click here and select the folder containing the page to which you want to link.

④ Click the file.

⑤ Click **OK**.

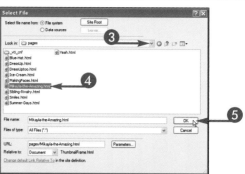

⑥ Click the **Target** ▾.

⑦ Click the name of the frame where you want the target file to open.

● Dreamweaver automatically names frames when they are created. Frame names are visible in the Frames panel.

⑧ Click 🌐 to preview the page in a Web browser.

Note: *To preview a page in a Web browser, see Chapter 2.*

When you open the framed page in a Web browser and click the link, the destination page opens inside the targeted frame.

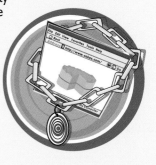

How do I create a link that opens a new page, outside of the frameset?

When you target a link, you can click **_top** from the Link drop-down menu in the Property inspector, instead of a frame name, to open the linked page in its own new browser window. This action takes the user out of the frameset, and is especially recommended when linking to another Web site.

Can I target a link to another Web site?

Yes. You can create a link to another Web site from a framed page by entering the URL in the Link field in the Property inspector. However, use this feature with care. Many Web site owners consider it bad form to display their Web pages within the frames on your Web site. Also, framing other Web sites can be confusing to visitors.

Format Frame Borders

You can modify the appearance of your frame borders to make them complement your design. One way is to specify the color and width of your borders. You can also turn them off so that they are not visible.

Format Frame Borders

SET BORDER SHADING, COLOR, AND WIDTH

1. Click the corner of an outside frame border to select the entire frameset.

2. Click here and select **Yes** or **Default** to turn on borders.

3. Type a border width in pixels.

4. Click the **Border color** ☐ (⟨ changes to ⟨).

5. Click a color.

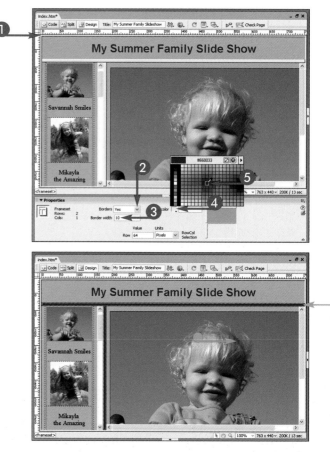

● The frame border appears at the specified settings.

You can override the frameset settings at the individual frame level if you want to change the settings to alter the border size or color of a single frame.

Click in the corresponding frame area in the Frames panel to select an individual frame. Then change the settings in the Property inspector.

TURN OFF BORDERS

1 Click the corner of an outside frame border to select the entire frameset.

2 Click the **Borders** ☑.

3 Click **No**.

4 Click 🌐 to preview the page in a Web browser.

Note: To preview a page in a Web browser, see Chapter 2.

● The frame border does not display.

Scroll bars display if they have not been turned off.

Links open in the targeted frame, even with borders turned off.

TIPS

Why would I want to make my frame borders invisible?

Turning borders off can disguise the fact that you are using frames in the first place. If you want to further disguise your frames, you can set the pages inside your frames to the same background color. To change background colors, see Chapter 6.

What if the frames do not look right in a Web browser when I preview them?

Because pages can display differently in different Web browsers than in Dreamweaver, you may want to make some adjustments to your frames after previewing them. If you find that the content is not exactly where you want it, or if there are other problems with your frames, then simply return to Dreamweaver, click and drag to adjust frame borders, and make any necessary adjustments to your content.

Control Scroll Bars in Frames

You can control whether or not scroll bars appear in your frames. Although hiding scroll bars enables you to have more control over the presentation of your Web site, it can also prevent some users from seeing your entire Web site content.

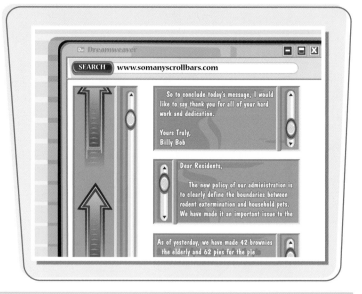

Control Scroll Bars in Frames

① Click a frame in the Frames panel to select it.

② Click the **Scroll** ▾.

③ Click a Scroll setting.

You can click **Yes** to keep scroll bars on, **No** to turn scroll bars off, or **Auto** to keep scroll bars on when necessary.

In most Web browsers, Default and Auto settings have the same result.

● The frame appears with the new setting.

In this example, scroll bars are turned off in the main frame.

By default, most browsers allow users to resize frames by clicking and dragging frame borders.

You can prevent users from resizing the frames of a Web site. However, depending on the size of their monitor, this may make it impossible for them to view all of your content.

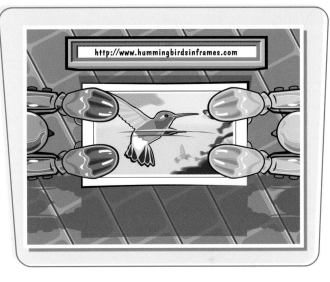

Control Resizing in Frames

① In the Frames panel, click a frame to select it.

② Click the **No resize** check box to remove the check mark if one is visible (☑ changes to ☐).

③ Click 🔍 to preview the page in a Web browser.

Note: To preview a page in a Web browser, see Chapter 2.

● The browser allows the user to resize the frame.

When you select the **No resize** check box, the browser prevents the user from resizing the frame.

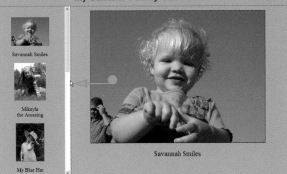

Creating Web-Based Forms

You can allow your Web site visitors to send you information by creating forms on your Web pages. This chapter shows you how to create forms with different types of fields, buttons, and menus.

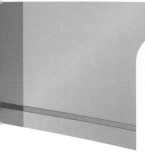

Introduction to Forms

You can add forms to your Web site to make it more interactive, thus allowing viewers to enter and submit information to you through your Web pages.

Forms work in conjunction with a program or script that processes the form information. Programmers generally create form scripts, and some scripts may be available through your service provider.

Create a Form

You can use Dreamweaver to construct a form by inserting text fields, drop-down menus, check boxes, and other interactive elements into your page. You can also enter the Web address of a form handler, or script, in Dreamweaver so that the information can be processed. Visitors to your Web page fill out the form and send the information to the script on your server by clicking a Submit button.

Process Form Information

Form handlers or scripts are programs that process the form information and execute an action, such as forwarding the information to an e-mail address or entering the contents of a form into a database. Although many ready-made form handlers are available for free on the Web, they generally require some customization. Your Web-hosting company may have forms available for you to use with your site. You can often find them by searching your hosting company's Web site or by calling tech support.

Define a Form Area

You can set up a form on your Web page by first creating a form container. The form container defines the area of the form where you place any text fields, menus, or other form elements. You associate the script or form handler by typing the name in the Property inspector.

Define a Form Area

① Click where you want to insert your form.

② Click **Insert**.

③ Click **Form**.

④ Click **Form**.

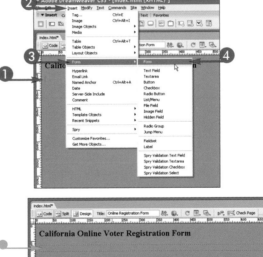

● A box appears, indicating that the form container is set up. To build the form, you can add form elements inside the red box.

⑤ Type the form address, which is determined by the location of the script on your Web server.

⑥ Click ☑.

⑦ Click either **POST** or **GET**.

Your selection should be based on the command that is required by the script or form handler that you are using.

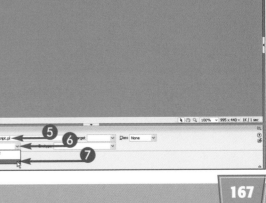

Add a Text Field to a Form

You can add a text field to enable viewers to submit text through your form. Text fields are probably the most common form element, enabling users to enter names, addresses, brief answers to questions, and other short pieces of text.

Add a Text Field to a Form

1 Click inside the form container where you want to insert the text field.

2 Click the **Forms tab**.

3 Click the **Text Field** icon ( ).

An Input Tag Accessibility Attributes dialog box appears.

4 Type a one-word ID.

5 Type a label.

6 Click **OK**.

● You can select the **Style** and **Position** attributes that you want (○ changes to ●).

● A text field appears in your form with the text that you entered in the Input Tag Accessibility Attributes dialog box.

● You can click Multi line (○ changes to ●) if you want a text box with more than one line available for text.

● You can change the assigned name of the text field.

7 Type an initial value for the text field if you want the text to appear in the form.

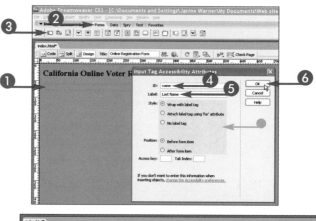

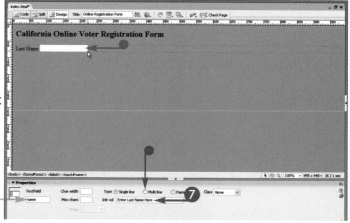

168

● The Initial value appears in the text field.

⑧ Type a character width to define the width of the text field.

⑨ Type a maximum number of characters to limit the amount of text that a user can enter.

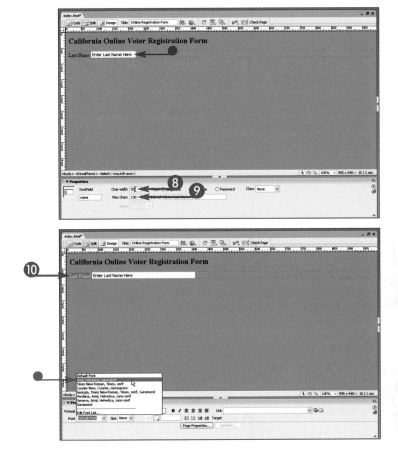

⑩ Click and drag to select a check box label.

● You can apply formatting options in the Property inspector.

Dreamweaver applies your specifications to the text field.

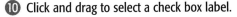

TIPS

Can I define the style of text that appears in the text field?

By default, the browser determines what style of text appears in form fields. It is not possible to format this type of text with plain HTML. You can use style sheets to manipulate the way the text in the form fields appears. However, keep in mind that only newer browsers support this formatting option. You can read more about style sheets in Chapter 12.

Can I create a text field with multiple lines?

Yes. When a text field has multiple lines, it is called a text area. You can insert a text area just as you insert a text field, by clicking the Text Field button (▭) in the Forms bar at the top of the screen.

Add a Check Box to a Form

Check boxes enable you to present multiple options in a form and allow the user to select one, several, or none of the options.

Add a Check Box to a Form

1. Click inside the form container where you want to insert the check box.

2. Click the **Forms tab**.

3. Click ☑ on the **Forms** bar.

   The Input Tag Accessibility Attributes dialog box appears.

4. Type a one-word ID.

5. Type a label.

6. Click **OK**.

Note: You can select the Style and Position attributes that you want (○ changes to ◉).

● The check box and label appear on the page.

7. Repeat Steps **3** to **6** until you have the number of check boxes that you want in your form.

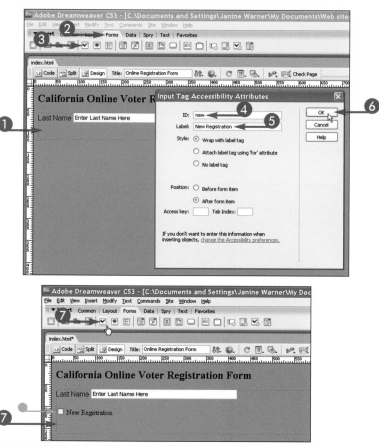

8 Click a check box to select it.

9 Click to select an Initial state option (◯) changes to (◉)).

You should specify other attributes in the Property inspector, such as the Checked value, based on the form handler or script that you are using.

10 Click to select the other check boxes in the group, one at a time, and specify attributes.

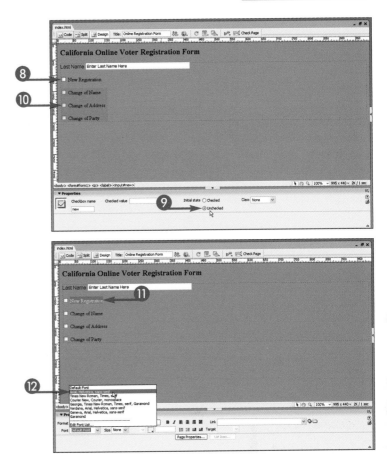

11 Click and drag to select a check box label.

12 Format the text using the Property inspector.

Dreamweaver applies your formatting to the label.

When should I use check boxes?

Check boxes are ideal when you want visitors to be able to select more than one option. Keep in mind that you may want to include the message, "Check all that apply."

When should I use radio buttons?

When you want visitors to select only one option from a list of two or more options, radio buttons are the best choice. You can set up your radio buttons so that it is not possible to select more than one option.

Add a Radio Button to a Form

You can allow visitors to select one of several options by adding a set of radio buttons to your form. With radio buttons, a user cannot select more than one option from a set.

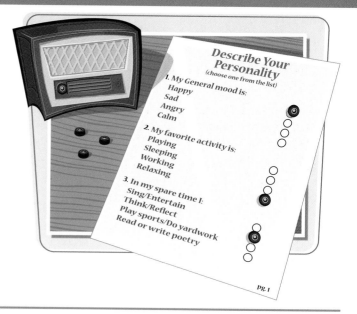

Add a Radio Button to a Form

1. Click inside the form container where you want to insert a radio button.

2. Click the **Radio Button** icon ([⊙]) on the Forms bar.

   The Input Tag Accessibility Attributes dialog box appears.

3. Type a one-word ID.

4. Type a label.

5. Click **OK**.

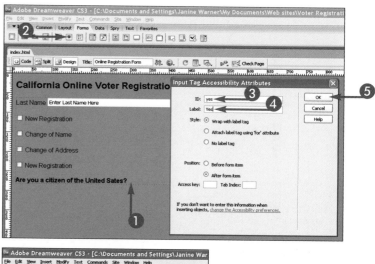

- A radio button and a label appear on the page.

6. Repeat Steps **2** to **5** until you have the number of radio buttons that you want in your form.

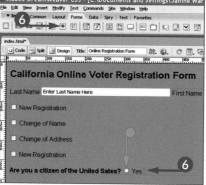

⑦ Click a radio button (⊙).

⑧ Click to select an Initial state option
(○ changes to ⊙).

You should specify other attributes in the Property inspector, such as the Checked value, based on the form handler or script that you are using.

⑨ Click to select the other radio buttons one at a time, and specify attributes for each radio button individually.

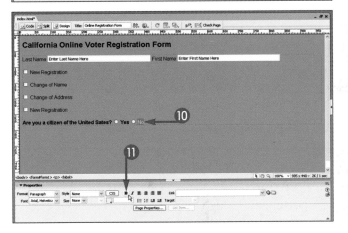

⑩ Click and drag to select radio button labels.

⑪ Format the text using the Property inspector.

Dreamweaver applies your formatting to the label.

TIPS

What happens if I give each radio button in a set a different name?

If you do this, then a user can select more than one button in the set at a time, and after a button is selected, the user cannot deselect it. This defeats the purpose of radio buttons. If you want to enable your users to select more than one choice or to deselect a choice, then you can use check boxes (☑) instead of radio buttons (⊙).

Are there alternatives to using check boxes or radio buttons?

Yes, there are alternatives such as menus and lists. Instead of using check boxes, you can use multi-select lists so that users can select more than one item from a list. You can replace a radio button with a menu that allows only one choice from a list.

Menus enable users to choose from a predefined list of choices. Similar to check boxes, users can choose one or more options from a menu or list.

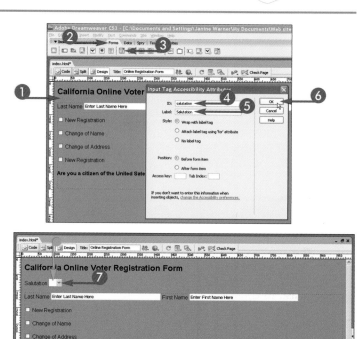

Add a Menu or List to a Form

1. Click inside the form container where you want a menu or list.

2. Click the **Forms** tab.

3. Click **List/Menu** (▤) on the Forms bar.

   The Input Tag Accessibility Attributes dialog box appears.

4. Type a one-word ID.

5. Type a label.

6. Click **OK**.

Note: You can select the Style and Position attributes that you want (◯ changes to ◉).

● A blank menu appears in your form.

7. Click the menu to select it.

8. Click **List Values**.

A List Values dialog box appears.

9 Type an Item Label and a Value for each menu item.

● You can click ⊞ or ⊟ to add or delete entries.

● You can select an item and click ▼ or ▲ to reposition the item in the list.

10 Click **OK** when you are done.

The entered values appear in the List box.

11 Click the item that you want to appear preselected when the page loads.

Dreamweaver applies your specifications to the menu.

TIPS

What determines the width of a menu or list?

The widest item determines the width of your menu or list. To change the width of the menu, you can change the width of your item descriptions.

Can I choose more than one item from a menu?

You can only select one item from a menu because of its design. If you want more than one selection, use a list and set it to allow multiple selections. You can also set the height greater than 1 so that you can see your selections.

Add a Submit Button to a Form

At the end of your form, you need to add a Submit button. This enables users to send the information that they have entered into the form to the specified script or form handler.

Add a Submit Button to a Form

1. Click inside the form container where you want to add the Submit button.

2. Click the **Forms** tab.

3. Click **Create** (🔲) on the Forms bar.

   The Input Tag Accessibility Attributes dialog box appears.

4. Type a one-word ID.

5. Type a label.

6. Click **OK**.

Note: You can select the Style and Position attributes that you want (◯ changes to ◉).

● A Submit button appears in the form.

7. Click the button to select it.

8. Type a value for the button.

   The text on the button changes from Submit to the value that you entered.

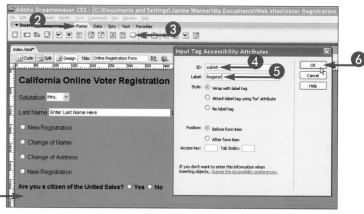

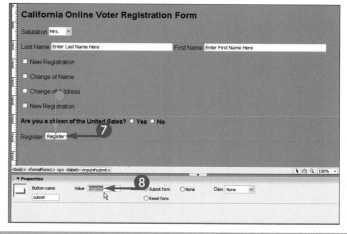

Add a Reset Button to a Form

You can add a Reset button to a form to enable users to erase their form entries so that they can start over.

Add a Reset Button to a Form

① Click inside the form container where you want to add the Reset button.

② Click the **Forms tab**.

③ Click (▢) on the Forms bar.

The Input Tag Accessibility Attributes dialog box appears.

④ Type a one-word ID.

⑤ Type a label.

⑥ Click **OK**.

Note: *You can select the Style and Position attributes that you want (○ changes to ●).*

● A Reset button appears in the form.

⑦ Click the button to select it.

⑧ Click the **Reset form** radio button (○ changes to ●).

● The Value automatically changes to Reset and the text on the button changes from Submit to Reset.

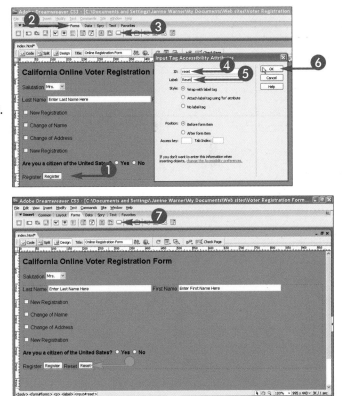

Using Library Items and Templates

You can save time by storing frequently used Web page elements and layouts as library items, and saving complete page designs as templates. This chapter shows you how to use these features to quickly create consistent page designs and make global updates.

Introduction to Library Items and Templates

With library items and templates, you can avoid repetitive work by storing copies of page elements and layouts that you frequently use. You can access the library items and templates that you create through the Assets panel.

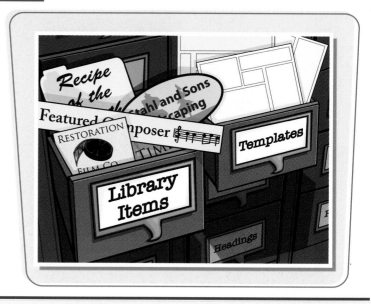

Library Items

You can define parts of your Web pages that are repeated in your Web site as library items. This saves you time because whenever you need a library item, you can just insert it from the Asset panel instead of re-creating it. If you make changes to a library item, then Dreamweaver automatically updates all instances of the item across your Web site. Good candidates for library items include advertising banners, company slogans, navigation bars, and any other feature that appears many times across your Web site.

Templates

You can define entire Web pages as templates to save you time as you build new pages. Templates can also help you maintain a consistent page design throughout a Web site. After you make changes to a template, Dreamweaver automatically updates all of the pages in your Web site that were created from that template. When you use templates, you customize only the areas of the page that you want to change.

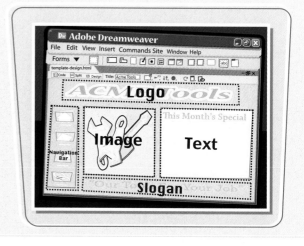

You can access the library and templates of a Web site by using commands in the Window menu. You can also access them through the Assets panel.

View Library Items and Templates

VIEW THE LIBRARY

1 Click **Window**.

2 Click **Assets**.

● The Assets panel opens.

3 Click the **Library** icon (📖) to view the library items.

● The Library window opens in the Assets panel.

VIEW TEMPLATES

1 Click **Window**.

2 Click **Assets**.

● The Assets panel opens.

3 Click the **Template** icon (📄) to view the templates.

● The Templates window opens in the Assets panel.

You can save text, links, images, and other elements as library items. A navigation row is a great example of content that works well as a library item. This is because you can save a collection of images, text, and links that you can quickly insert into other pages without having to re-create them.

If you edit a library item, Dreamweaver automatically updates each instance of the item throughout your Web site.

Create a Library Item

① Click and drag to select an element or collection of elements that you want to define as a library item.

Note: Before you can use the library item feature in Dreamweaver, you must first set up and define your local site. To set up a local site, see Chapter 2.

② Click **Modify**.

③ Click **Library**.

④ Click **Add Object to Library**.

● A new untitled library item appears in the Library window.

⑤ Type a name for the library item.

⑥ Press **Enter** (**Return**).

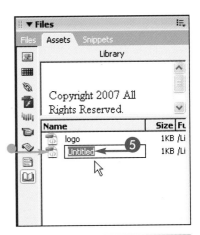

The named library item appears in the Assets panel.

Defining an element as a library item prevents you from editing it in the Document window.

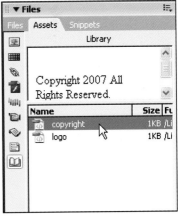

What page elements should I make into library items?

Anything that appears multiple times in a Web site is a good candidate to become a library item. These elements include headers, footers, navigational menus, contact information, and disclaimers. Any element that appears in the body of an HTML document, including text, images, tables, forms, layers, and multimedia, may be defined as a library item.

Can I use multiple library items on the same HTML page?

There is no limit to the number of library items that you can use on a page. If your Web site is very standardized, then there may be little on your page that is not a library item. For example, you can create a photo gallery where each page has the same layout, except for the photo.

Insert a Library Item

You can insert an element onto your page from the Library to avoid having to create it yourself. This also ensures that the element is identical to other instances of that library item in your Web site.

Insert a Library Item

① Click **Window**.

② Click **Assets**.

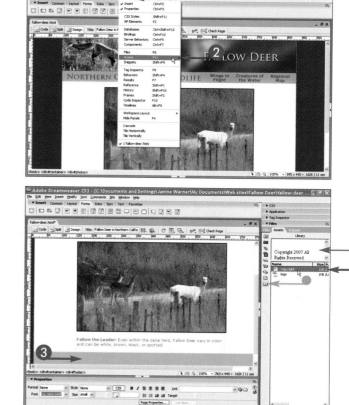

The Assets panel opens.

● If the Library window is not open in the Assets panel, you can click 🔲 to view it.

③ Position ▷ where you want to insert the library item.

④ Click a library item.

● The library item appears in the top of the Library window.

5 Right-click the library item.

6 Click **Insert**.

You can also click and drag library items from the Library window to the page to insert them.

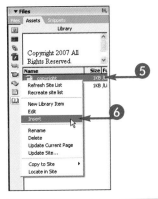

● Dreamweaver inserts the library item in the Document window.

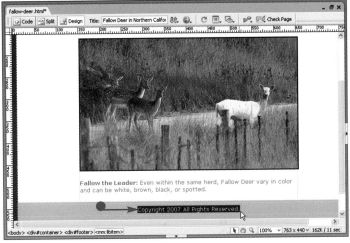

Fallow the Leader: Even within the same herd, Fallow Deer vary in color and can be white, brown, black, or spotted.

Copyright 2007 All Rights Reserved

Edit and Update a Library Item to Your Web Site

You can edit a library item and then automatically update all of the pages in your Web site that feature that item. This feature can help you save time when updating or redesigning a Web site.

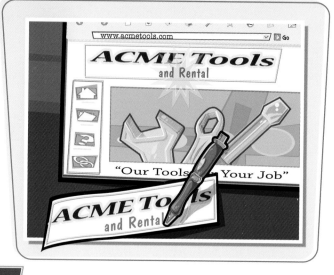

Edit and Update a Library Item to Your Web Site

Note: *If the Assets panel is not open, see the task, "View Library Items and Templates."*

1. Double-click a library item to open it.

   The library item opens in a new window.

2. Edit any element in the library item.

   You can add or delete text, or insert tables.

   In this example, the year 2007 is changed to 2008 in the copyright library item.

3. Click **File**.

4. Click **Save**.

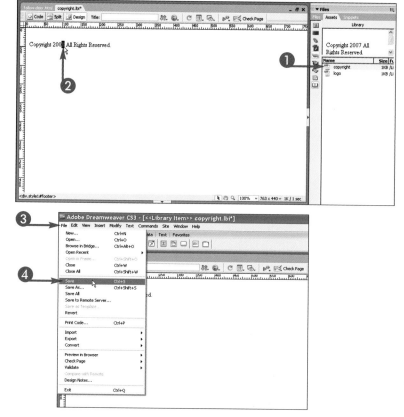

The Update Library Items dialog box appears, asking if you want to update all instances of the library item in the site.

⑤ Click **Update**.

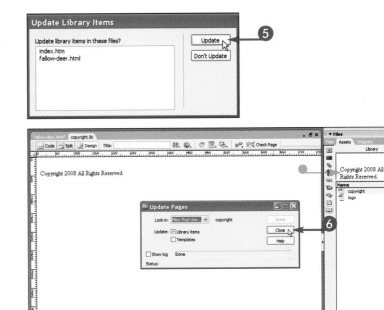

The Update Pages dialog box appears, showing the progress of the updates.

⑥ After Dreamweaver updates the site, click **Close**.

All pages where the library item appears are updated.

● Changes are also made to the stored library item and are visible in the Assets panel.

 TIPS

What do my pages look like after I have edited a library item and updated my Web site?

When you edit a library item and choose to update any instances of the library item that are already inserted into your Web pages, all of those instances are replaced with the edited versions. By using the library feature, you can make a change to a single library item and have multiple Web pages updated automatically.

Can I undo an update to a library item?

Technically, no. When you update pages with the library feature, the Undo command does not undo all of the instances of these changes. However, you can go back to the Assets panel, open the library item, change it back to the way it was, and then apply those changes to all of the pages again.

Detach Library Content for Editing

You can detach an inserted library item from the original stored library item and then edit it as you would any other element in a Web page. If you detach a library item, then you can no longer make automatic updates when you change the original stored library item.

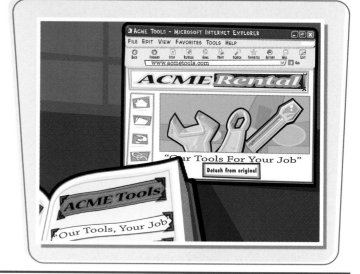

Detach Library Content for Editing

1 Click to select the library item that you want to edit independently.

2 Click **Detach from original**.

A warning dialog box appears.

3 Click **OK**.

● You can stop the warning from appearing each time you perform this action by clicking the **Don't warn me again** check box (☐ changes to ☑).

The element is no longer a library item and has no distinctive highlighting.

④ Click where you want to edit the library item, and make any edits that you want.

● You can add, delete, and format text. In this example, the font is changed.

● Dreamweaver applies the editing to the text, image, or other element within the page.

Note: Editing a detached library item has no effect on library items that are used on other pages.

When would I use the Detach from Original command?

This command is useful when you use library items as partial page templates for specific design elements. For example, if you plan to have many captioned images in your Web site, you can create a library item with a two-celled table that contains a generic image and a formatted text caption. As a result, rather than re-creating the table every time you want to add an image, you can insert the library item and then detach it from the library to make it editable. You can then replace the generic image and caption with appropriate content, as the formatting and design are done for you.

Can you reattach a library item?

Not exactly, but you can always reinsert a library item into a page and then delete the unattached library item. As a result, any changes that you make to the stored version are applied to the newly inserted version. Inserting a library item again may be faster than making the updates manually.

Create a Template

Templates are one of the most powerful and timesaving features in Dreamweaver because they enable you to create page designs that can be reused over and over again. Templates can also help you create more consistent designs for your pages.

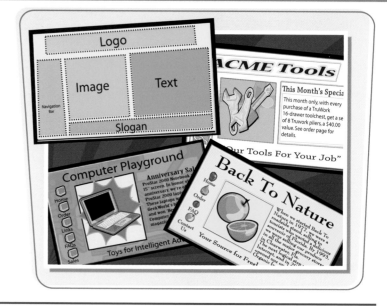

Create a Template

Note: *To create templates for your Web pages, you must already have defined a local Web site. To set up a local Web site, see Chapter 2.*

① Create and design a new page, or open the page that serves as a template.

● You can add placeholders where information changes from page to page.

② Click **File**.

③ Click **Save as Template**.

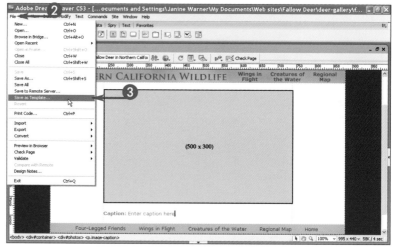

The Save As Template dialog box appears.

④ Click here and select your site name.

⑤ Type a name for the template.

⑥ Click **Save**.

Save As Template

Site: Fallow Deer ④

Existing templates: blacktail-deer

Description:

Save as: fallow-deer ⑤

Save ⑥

Cancel

Help

● The new template appears in the Templates window of the Assets panel.

If a template folder does not already exist, Dreamweaver automatically creates one to which it saves the new template.

Note: To make the template functional, you must define the editable regions where you want to modify content. For more information, see the task, "Set an Editable Region in a Template."

▼ Files

Files | Assets | Snippets

Templates

Name	Size	Fu
blacktail-deer	3KB	/Ti
fallow-deer	3KB	/T

TIPS

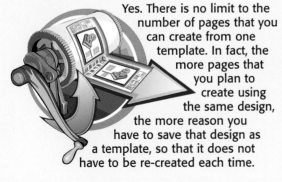

Can I create as many pages as I want from a template?

Yes. There is no limit to the number of pages that you can create from one template. In fact, the more pages that you plan to create using the same design, the more reason you have to save that design as a template, so that it does not have to be re-created each time.

How do you edit a page that is created with a template?

After you create a new Web page based on a template, you can only change the parts of the new page that are defined as editable. To change locked content, you must edit the original template. For more information about creating editable regions in a template, see the task, "Set an Editable Region in a Template."

Set an Editable Region in a Template

After you create a Web page template, you must define which regions of the template are editable. When you create a page from the template, you can then edit these regions. Any areas of the template that are not set as editable cannot be changed in any pages that you create from the template.

Set an Editable Region in a Template

① Click **Window**.

② Click **Assets**.

The Files panel appears with the Assets tab visible.

③ Click **Templates** (🖿).

④ Double-click a template name to open it.

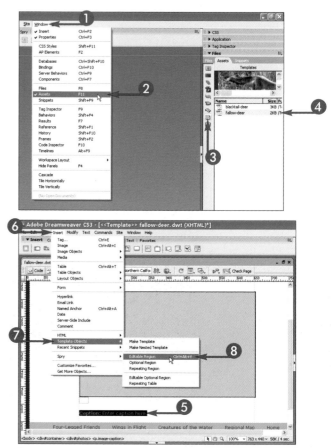

The template opens in the work area.

⑤ Click and drag to select the element that you want to define as editable.

⑥ Click **Insert**.

⑦ Click **Template Objects**.

⑧ Click **Editable Region**.

The New Editable Region dialog box appears.

⑨ Type a name for the editable region that distinguishes it from other editable regions on the page.

Note: You cannot use the characters &, ", ', <, or > in the name.

⑩ Click **OK**.

● A light-blue box indicates the editable region, and a tab shows the region name.

⑪ Repeat Steps **5** to **10** for all of the regions on the page that you want to be editable.

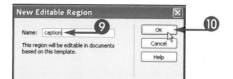

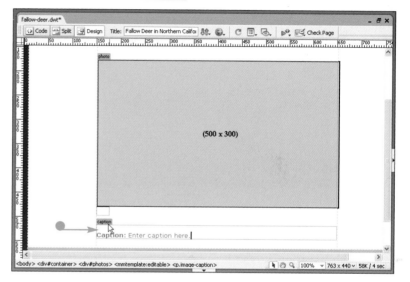

What parts of a template should be defined as editable?

You should define as editable any part of your template that you want to change from page to page. This can include headlines, stories, images, and captions. In contrast, you should lock site navigation, disclaimers, and copyright information that should be the same on all pages.

Can I use library items in my template pages?

Yes, you can use library items in templates. This is useful when you want to insert an item on pages that are made from the template. When you edit them, the library items update in the actual templates, and then in all of the pages that are created from those templates.

Create a Page from a Template

You can create a new Web page based on a template that you have already defined. This step saves you from having to rebuild all of the generic elements that appear on many of your pages.

Create a Page from a Template

① Click **File**.

② Click **New**.

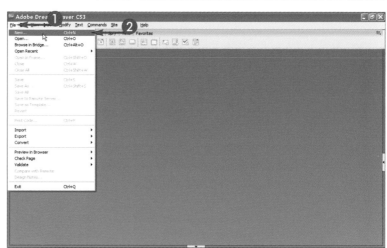

The New Document dialog box appears.

③ Click the **Page from Template** tab.

④ Click the name of the Web site.

⑤ Click a template.

● A preview of the template appears in the dialog box.

⑥ Click **Create**.

Dreamweaver generates a new page from the template.

● The editable regions are surrounded by blue boxes.

7 Type content into the editable regions.

8 Insert images into the editable regions.

Note: Only editable areas can be altered in a page created from a template.

9 Click **File**.

10 Click **Save** to save the template.

Dreamweaver saves the new page, based on the template.

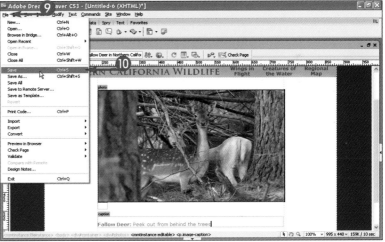

TIP

How do I detach a page from a template?

1 Click **Modify**.

2 Click **Templates**.

3 Click **Detach from Template**.

The page becomes a regular document with previously locked regions now fully editable. Edits to the original template no longer update the page.

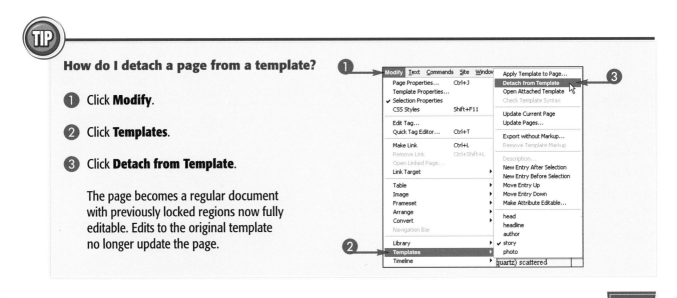

Edit a Template and Update Your Web Site

When you make updates to a template file, Dreamweaver allows you the option to automatically update all of the pages that are created by the template. This enables you to make global changes to your Web site design in seconds.

Edit a Template and Update Your Web Site

① Click **Window**.

② Click **Assets**.

The Files panel appears with the Assets tab visible.

③ Click 🖼.

The available templates appear.

④ Double-click a template to open it.

⑤ Click in an area of the template that is not an editable region.

Note: *Only locked regions of a template can be used to make updates to pages created from the template.*

● In this example, the copyright date is changed from 2007 to 2008.

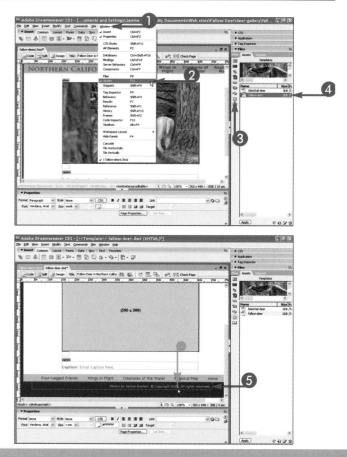

⑥ Press `Ctrl` (`⌘`)+`S` to save the page.

The Update Template Files dialog box appears, listing all files based on the selected template that will be updated.

⑦ Click **Update**.

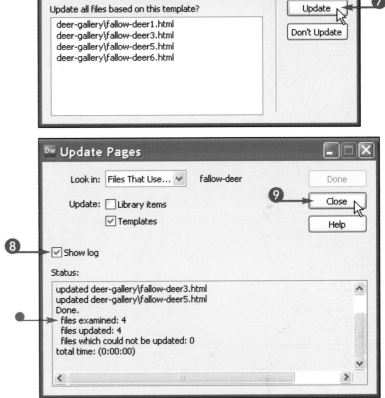

Update Template Files

Update all files based on this template?

deer-gallery\fallow-deer1.html
deer-gallery\fallow-deer3.html
deer-gallery\fallow-deer5.html
deer-gallery\fallow-deer6.html

Update ⑦
Don't Update

The Update Pages dialog box appears.

⑧ Click the **Show log** check box (☐ changes to ☑).

● The results of the update process appear in the Status pane.

⑨ After Dreamweaver updates the Web site, click **Close**.

All of the pages that use the template are updated to reflect the changes.

Dw Update Pages

Look in: Files That Use... ✓   fallow-deer   Done

Update: ☐ Library items   ⑨→ Close

☑ Templates   Help

⑧ ☑ Show log

Status:

updated deer-gallery\fallow-deer3.html
updated deer-gallery\fallow-deer5.html
Done.
  files examined: 4
  files updated: 4
  files which could not be updated: 0
total time: (0:00:00)

TIPS

How does Dreamweaver store page templates?

Dreamweaver stores page templates in a folder called Templates inside the local site folder. You can open templates by clicking **File** and then clicking **Open**. In the Open dialog box, click ☑ and click the **Template** folder. You can click a template file to select it. You can also open templates from inside the Assets panel.

What are editable attributes?

Editable attributes enable you to change the attributes of an element in the Property inspector. For example, you can change image attributes, such as Alternative text, alignment, or size. To use this feature, select an element, such as an image, click **Modify**, then click **Templates**, and then click **Make Attribute Editable**.

CHAPTER 12

Creating and Applying Cascading Style Sheets

This chapter shows you how to use Cascading Style Sheets to create and apply formatting. Cascading Style Sheets can save you a lot of tedious formatting time, especially if you format big Web sites.

Introduction to Cascading Style Sheets

You can apply many different types of formatting to your Web pages with style sheets, also known as Cascading Style Sheets, or CSS.

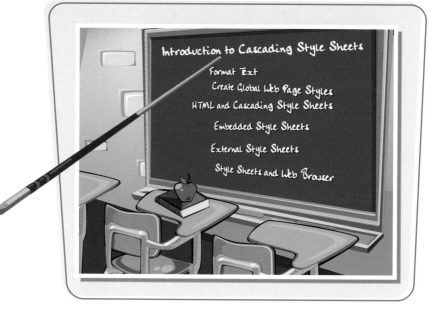

Format Text

CSS enables you to create as many different style sheets as you want. You can then use them to format text by applying multiple formatting options at once, such as the font face, size, and color.

Create Global Web Page Styles

You can create style sheets that apply to all of the pages in your Web site. You can then use the same style across your pages to make the formatting more consistent by saving the style in an external style sheet. You can even make global changes by editing a style sheet to change the style across all of the pages that link to the external style sheet.

Cascading Style Sheet Selectors

You can create styles by using the tag selector to redefine an existing HTML tag, or by using the class selector to create new class styles that can be applied to any element on a Web page.

Internal Style Sheets

A style sheet saved within the HTML code of a Web page is called an internal style sheet. Internal style sheet rules apply only to the page in which they are included.

External Style Sheets

When you want your styles to apply to multiple pages on your Web site, you must save them in a separate file called an external style sheet. You can attach the same external style sheet to any or all of the pages in a Web site.

Style Sheets and Web Browsers

Some older Web browsers do not support style sheet standards, and different Web browsers display style sheets differently. Always test pages that use style sheets on different browsers to ensure that content displays as you intend it to for all of your visitors.

Customize an HTML Tag

You can customize the style that an existing HTML tag applies. This allows you to apply special formatting whenever you use that tag to format text. This is a quick, easy way to apply multiple style options with one HTML tag.

Not Customized <h1>   Customized <h1>

1 Click **Text**.

2 Click **CSS Styles**.

3 Click **New**.

The New CSS Rule dialog box appears.

4 Click the **Tag** option (○ changes to ◉).

5 Click here and select a tag.

6 Click **This document only** to create an embedded style sheet for the file on which you are working (○ changes to ◉).

Note: To create style sheets for more than one document, see the task, "Create an External Style Sheet."

7 Click **OK**.

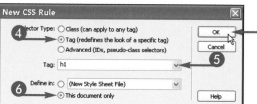

The CSS Rule Definition dialog box appears.

8 Click a style category.

9 Select the style settings that you want.

10 Click **OK**.

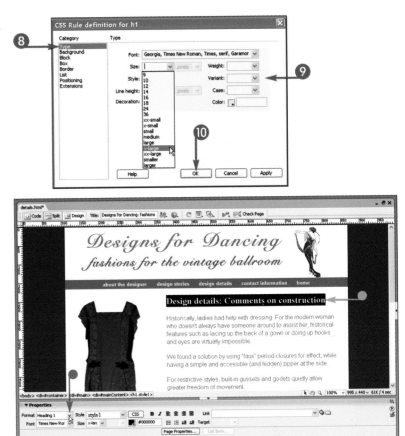

● Dreamweaver adds the new style to any content that is formatted with the redefined tag.

In this example, Heading 1 is redefined to use a different font face and size.

● You can also apply the style by selecting content on the page and selecting the Heading 1 format.

TIPS

Why should I redefine an HTML tag?

When you redefine an HTML tag, you can apply more than one style to the tag. As a result, you only have to use one HTML tag instead of several to apply multiple formatting options. For example, you can add center alignment to all of your H1 tags to control the alignment of heading styles in one step. A special advantage to redefining HTML tags is that if a user's Web browser does not support style sheets, then the HTML tag still provides its basic formatting.

Does redefining an HTML tag change the format of any content that uses that tag?

Yes. When you redefine an HTML tag, you change the tag's formatting effect anywhere that you use the tag. You can limit the change to the page that you are working on, or you can include it in an external style sheet and apply it to an entire site. If you do not want to alter the style of an existing HTML tag, then you should create class style sheets instead of redefining HTML tags. For more information on class style sheets, see the task, "Create a Class Style."

Create a Class Style

You can create class styles that can be used to format text and other elements on a Web page without affecting HTML tags. You can then apply those styles to any elements on your Web page, much like you would apply an HTML tag.

Create a Class Style

1. Click **Text**.
2. Click **CSS Styles**.
3. Click **New**.

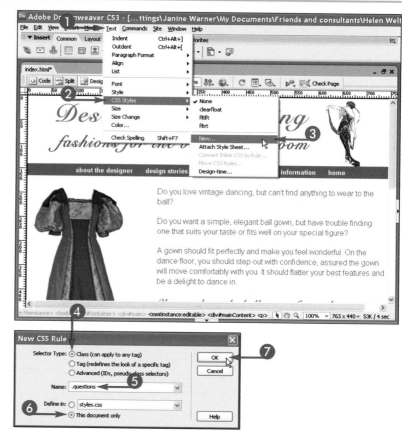

The New CSS Rule dialog box appears.

4. Click **Class** (◯ changes to ◉).
5. Type a name for the style.

Note: Class style names must begin with a period (.).

6. Click **This document only** (◯ changes to ◉).

Note: To create style sheets for more than one document, see the section, "Create an External Style Sheet."

7. Click **OK**.

The CSS Rule Definition dialog box appears.

8 Click a style category.

9 Select the style settings that you want.

10 Click **OK**.

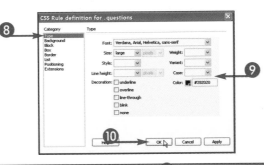

The CSS Rule Definition dialog box closes.

11 Click **Window**.

12 Click **CSS Styles**.

● The CSS Styles panel opens, displaying the new class style.

In this example, text style options are used to change the font face, color, and size. You can apply the class style to new or existing content.

Note: *To apply a new class style, see the section, "Apply a Class Style."*

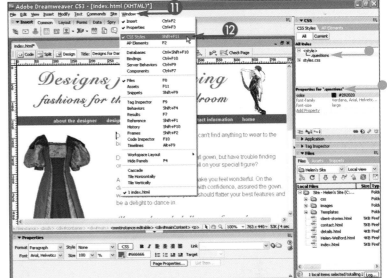

How does customizing an HTML tag differ from creating a custom style?

Customizing an HTML tag links a style to an existing HTML tag. The new style affects every instance of that tag. For example, if you customize your H1 tags as green, then every time you use the H1 tag to format a headline, the text will be green. With class styles, you can apply styles that are independent of HTML tags and use them only where you want them.

Is it better to customize an HTML tag or create my own custom styles?

One of the benefits of redefining existing HTML tags is that you can take advantage of recognized styles and hierarchies. This is especially true with heading tags. For example, if you change the way H1, H2, and H3 tags appear, it is best to maintain their relative size difference, keeping H1 as the largest and using it to format the most important heading on the page.

Apply a Class Style

You can apply a class style to any element on your Web page. Class styles allow you to change color, font, size, alignment, and other characteristics. You can use the same class style multiple times on the same page.

APPLY A CLASS STYLE TO TEXT

Note: *To create a new custom style, see the section, "Create a Class Style."*

① Click and drag to select the text to which you want to apply a style.

② In the Property inspector, click the **Style** ☑.

③ Click the name of a style.

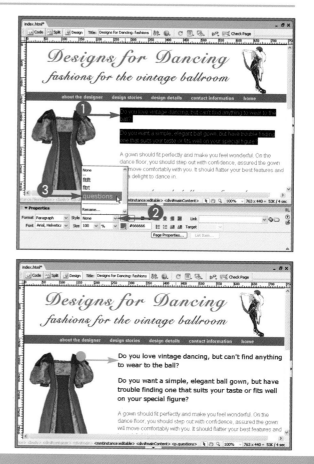

● Dreamweaver applies the style.

In this example, a font style is applied.

APPLY A CLASS STYLE TO AN IMAGE

Note: To create a new custom style, see the section, "Create a Class Style."

1 Click to select an image.

2 In the Property inspector, click the **Style** ☑.

3 Click the name of the style.

● Dreamweaver applies the new style sheet to the entire body of the page in the Document window.

In this example, the image is aligned to the right, and 8 pixels of margin space are added to the left side of the image.

TIPS

What are some other options that I can use to define the formatting for text with a style sheet?

With style sheets, you can specify a numeric value for font weight. This enables you to apply varying degrees of boldness, instead of just a single boldness setting as with HTML. You can also define type size in absolute units, such as pixels, points, picas, inches, centimeters, or millimeters, or in relative units, such as ems, exes, or percentage.

Can I create as many style sheets as I want?

Yes. However, one of the goals of style sheets is to help you work more efficiently, so you should generally use them for formatting options that you want to apply many times within a document or Web site.

Style Sheet
heading 1
image
heading 2 paragraph
image

You can edit style sheet definitions. You can then automatically apply the changes across all of the text or other elements to which you have applied the style on your Web page or Web site.

Edit a Style

① Click **Window**.

② Click **CSS Styles**.

● The CSS Styles panel opens, displaying all of the available styles.

③ Double-click the name of a style that you want to edit.

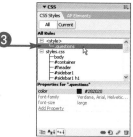

The CSS Rule Definition dialog box opens.

④ Click a style category.

⑤ Select the style settings that you want.

In this example, the font color is changed.

⑥ Click **OK**.

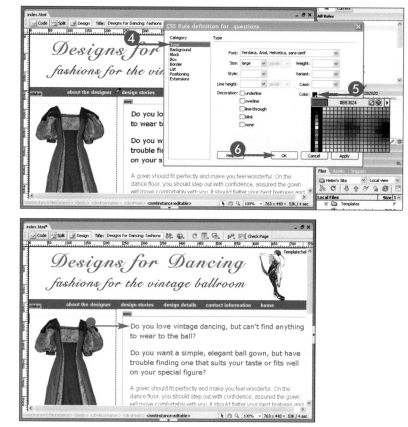

Dreamweaver saves the style sheet changes and automatically applies them anywhere that you have used the style.

● In this example, the font color changes automatically in the text where the style has already been applied.

TIP

How many different kinds of styles are there?

You can create multiple kinds of style rules, but the main options are tag styles, class styles, ID styles, and advanced styles. Tag styles are used to redefine HTML tags. Class styles are used to create new styles that can be applied to any element on a page and used multiple times. ID styles are designed to apply style information where an ID has been used to identify an element. ID styles are commonly used with DIV tags to control the placement of elements on a page and create page layouts.

Create Styles with Page Properties

You can use Dreamweaver's Page Properties dialog box to define page-wide styles, such as background colors, link styles, and text options.

When you define these options in the Page Properties dialog box, Dreamweaver automatically creates the corresponding styles and adds them to the Styles panel.

① Click the **Page Properties** button in the Property inspector.

The Page Properties dialog box appears.

② Click **Appearance**.

③ Select the font, size, color, and spacing you want.

④ Set page margins to 0 to remove the default indent in the left and top margins of the display area.

⑤ Click **Apply**.

⑥ Click **Links**.

⑦ Select font, size, and link colors.

⑧ Click here and select **Never Underline** to remove the underline style from all links on the page.

⑨ Click **Apply**.

⑩ Click **Headings**.

⑪ Select the font, size, and colors for each of the six heading styles.

⑫ Click **OK**.

● Dreamweaver saves the corresponding styles in the Styles panel.

● Dreamweaver automatically applies the new style information to the page.

Note: *To create style sheets for more than one document, see the section, "Create an External Style Sheet."*

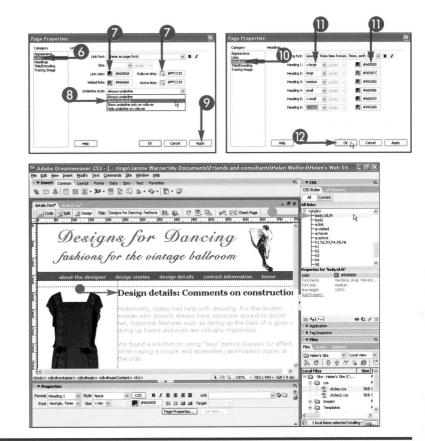

What are some non-text-based features that I can implement with style sheets?

Probably the most exciting thing that you can do with style sheets is to position elements precisely on the page. Style sheets allow you freedom from traditional, and imprecise, layout methods, such as HTML tables. Style sheets use the DIV tag, which defines an area on the page where you can position an element with alignment attributes. You can also position the element more precisely by specifying an actual pixel location in the page.

Do all Web browsers support CSS in the same way?

No, unfortunately not all Web browsers support CSS in the same way, and some do not support styles at all. However, styles have come a long way in the last few years, and so have browsers. Although some visitors may not be able to see your designs as you intend if you use CSS, the vast majority of people surfing the Web these days have browsers that support CSS.

Create an External Style Sheet

External style sheets enable you to define a set of style sheet rules and then apply them to many different pages — even pages on different Web sites. This allows you to keep a consistent appearance across many pages, and to streamline formatting and style updates.

Note: *Make sure the CSS Styles panel is open. Click Window, then click CSS Styles.*

① Click **New style** (▣).

The New CSS Rule dialog box appears.

② Click a style option (○ changes to ◉).

③ Type a name for the style or select a tag from the ▽.

④ Click **Define in** (○ changes to ◉).

⑤ Select **New Style Sheet File**.

You can also select any existing external style sheet.

⑥ Click **OK**.

⑦ Click here to select the folder where you want to save the new style sheet.

⑧ Type a name for the style sheet.

⑨ Click **Save**.

The CSS Rule Definition dialog box appears.

🔟 Click a category.

⓫ Select the style settings that you want.

⓬ Click **OK**.

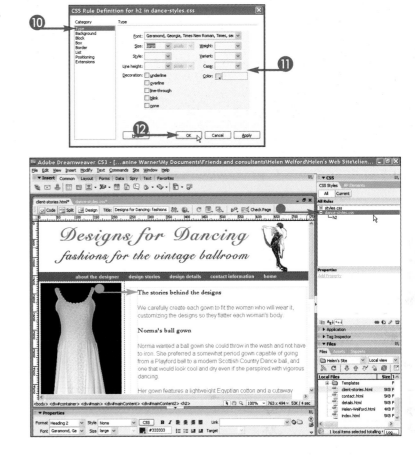

● Dreamweaver saves the style to the new external style sheet and attaches the new style sheet to the open page.

● The new style sheet displays in the CSS Styles panel.

Note: *The external style sheet is created inside your local site folder. For this to work, you must have defined your site in Dreamweaver. To define a site and identify the local site folder, see Chapter 2.*

TIPS

How can I add more styles to an external style sheet?

When you create any new style, you have the option of selecting an existing style sheet from the Define In field in the New CSS Rule dialog box. To create a class style, see the section, "Create a Class Style." To customize an HTML tag, see the section, "Customize an HTML Tag." When you define a new style in an external style, it is automatically added to the selected CSS file.

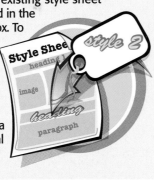

Is it possible to add new styles later?

Yes. You can add styles to an external style sheet at any point during production, even months after the site was first published. In addition, you can make changes or additions while you work on any page that is currently attached to an external style sheet, and those styles will become available on any page where the style sheet is attached.

Attach an External Style Sheet

Any style sheet that you create becomes accessible from the Property inspector Style field. Creating style sheets for common formatting options makes it easy to apply complicated styles with a single click. You must attach the style sheet first before you can apply the styles to the content on your page.

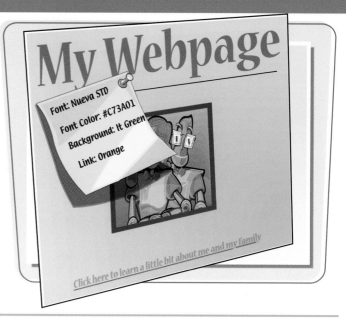

Attach an External Style Sheet

① In the page to which you want to attach a style sheet, click **Text**.

② Click **CSS Styles**.

③ Click **Attach Style Sheet**.

The Attach External Style Sheet dialog box appears.

④ Click **Browse**.

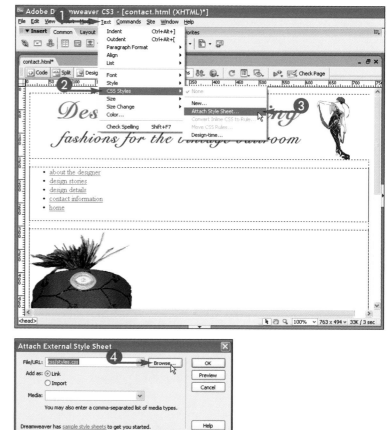

⑤ Click the name of the style sheet that you want to attach.

⑥ Click **OK**.

⑦ Click **OK**.

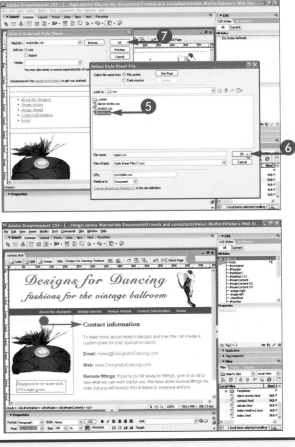

● The External Style Sheet is linked to the page, and the style sheet displays in the CSS panel.

● The styles from the external style sheet are automatically applied to the page.

Note: *To apply styles to content in a document, see the section, "Apply a Class Style."*

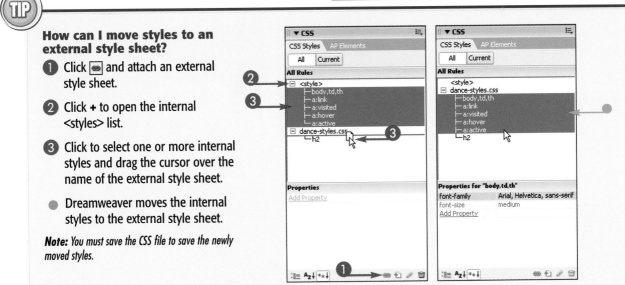

TIP

How can I move styles to an external style sheet?

① Click 🔲 and attach an external style sheet.

② Click + to open the internal <styles> list.

③ Click to select one or more internal styles and drag the cursor over the name of the external style sheet.

● Dreamweaver moves the internal styles to the external style sheet.

Note: *You must save the CSS file to save the newly moved styles.*

Edit an External Style Sheet

You can include hundreds of styles in a single external sheet. This allows you to continue to add to the style sheet as your site grows, and to change or add sections.

Edit an External Style Sheet

① Click **Window**.

② Click **CSS Styles**.

● The CSS panel appears.

● You can click here and drag to expand the CSS panel.

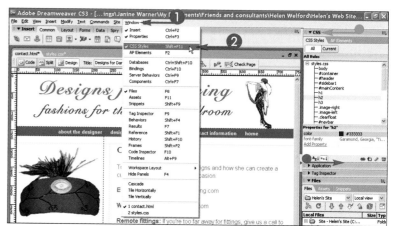

③ Double-click the name of a style.

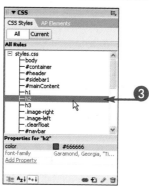

The CSS Rule Definition dialog box appears.

④ Click a style category.

⑤ Select the style settings that you want.

● In this example, the font color is changed.

⑥ Click **OK**.

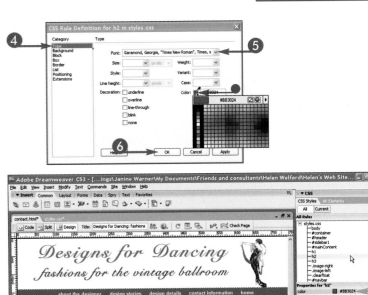

● Dreamweaver saves the new style definition in the external style sheet.

● The new style is automatically applied to any content on the page that is formatted with that style.

TIP

What problems can arise when I use CSS?

The benefits to using Cascading Style Sheets are enormous, and they mostly outweigh the challenges that come with their implementation. Because CSS does not display the same in all Web browsers, pages designed with CSS may not display the same on all computers. You should always test your pages to make sure that you like the results in all of the browsers that you expect your visitors to use. For best results, redefine existing HTML tags when possible and create your page designs so that they will be readable and display well, even if the styles are not supported.

Designing a Web Site with CSS

In addition to other layout options, Dreamweaver allows you to quickly create AP Divs. This chapter shows you how to gain more design control and increase user interaction using the AP Divs feature, as well as how to use Divs without absolute positioning to create centered designs.

You can use advanced Dreamweaver tools to create *AP Divs* and then stack them on top of each other for more precise layout control. You can also add scripting with Dreamweaver behaviors to increase the interactivity of your Web site.

AP Div Basics

AP Divs are discrete blocks of content that you can precisely position on the page, make moveable by the user, and even make invisible. Most significantly, you can stack AP Divs on top of each other. AP Divs can contain any kind of content, including text, graphics, tables, and even other AP Divs. Unfortunately, because AP Divs are so new to HTML, they are not supported in the same way by all Web browsers, and so you may need to do more testing to ensure that your pages work properly.

Nested AP Divs

AP Divs can contain nested AP Divs, which create areas of content that stay linked together on a page for better control during production of Web pages. *Nested,* or child, AP Divs can inherit the properties of their parent AP Divs, including visibility or invisibility. You can also nest AP Divs within other nested AP Divs.

Behavior Basics

Behaviors are cause-and-effect events that you can insert into your Web pages. For example, you can use the Swap Image behavior to make pictures on a Web page change, or the Open Browser Window behavior to cause a new Web browser window to open when a user clicks or moves a mouse over an image or other element on a Web page.

Behaviors and Browsers

Because behaviors vary in complexity, they are written in various ways to ensure compatibility with older Web browsers. The latest versions of both Internet Explorer and Firefox display most of Dreamweaver's behaviors well, and you can disable behaviors that may not work in older Web browsers.

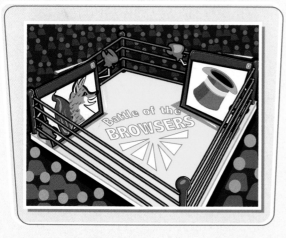

Behind the Scenes

Dreamweaver creates most behaviors with JavaScript, but some Behaviors use ActiveX and SSI. JavaScript is by far the most accepted and widely used browser-side programming language due to its wide acceptance, versatility, and powerful capabilities.

Creating Centered CSS Designs

AP Divs offer one of the easiest options for creating intricate Web designs, but because they use absolute positioning, they are fixed on the page and cannot be centered within a browser window. To create centered designs, you can use DIV tags without absolute positioning by creating CSS styles to control the display of your page elements. Dreamweaver CS3 features many new CSS layouts to make it easier to use this complex design option.

Create an AP Div with Content

AP Divs are scalable rectangles, inside of which you can place text, images, and just about anything else you can include in a Web page. Although they work similarly to tables by providing design control, they are much more precise and much more intuitive to use because you can simply click and drag to create an AP Div anywhere on a page.

Create an AP Div with Content

CREATE AN AP DIV

① Click the **Layout** tab in the Insert bar.

② Click **Draw AP Div** (⬚).

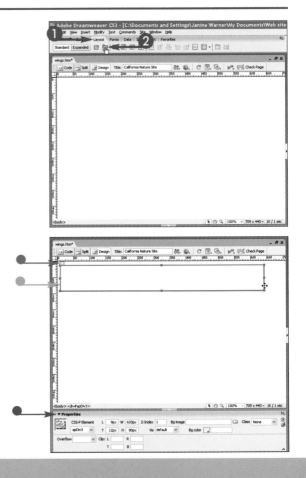

③ Click and drag to create an AP Div in the page.

  You can resize and reposition an AP Div after you create it.

● The outline of the AP Div appears.

● You can click the tab in the upper-left corner of the AP Div to select it.

● When you select the AP Div, the Property inspector displays the AP Div's properties.

ADD CONTENT TO AN AP DIV

1 Click inside the AP Div (☝ changes to ⌶).

2 Click to select an image in the Files panel and drag it into the AP Div (☝ changes to ⬚).

You can also add text by typing inside an AP Div. You can format text and images within an AP Div using the Property inspector, just as you would format text or images anywhere else on a page.

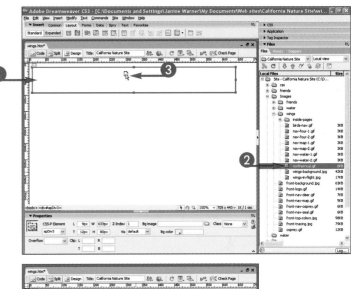

● The image displays inside the AP Div.

You can specify image properties, such as alignment, within an AP Div by clicking to select the image and changing the image properties in the Property inspector.

Note: To format text, see Chapter 5. For image options, see Chapter 6.

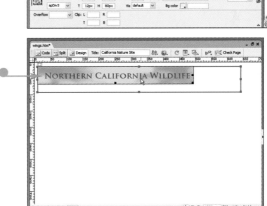

NORTHERN CALIFORNIA WILDLIFE

 TIPS

Should I use AP Divs instead of HTML tables?

AP Divs are very powerful layout tools that offer a page designer better control over the placement of content on a Web page. However, AP Divs are not fully supported by all Web browsers, so many Web designers continue to use tables to create page designs. If you use AP Divs, your pages may display differently in different browsers.

What happens if a browser does not support AP Divs?

Although the latest versions of Internet Explorer and Firefox support AP Divs, older browsers that do not support AP Divs simply ignore them. Unfortunately, this means that if someone views your page using an older browser, then any content, such as text or images, that you place inside an AP Div, is not visible.

Resize and Reposition AP Divs

When you create a new AP Div, you can adjust its position and dimensions to make it fit attractively within the rest of the content on your page. One of the advantages of AP Divs is that you can move them easily, by clicking and dragging them.

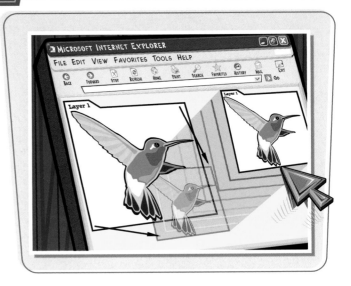

CLICK AND DRAG TO RESIZE AN AP DIV

1 Click the tab in the upper-left corner of the AP Div to select it.

● Square, black handles appear around the edges of the AP Div.

2 Click and drag one of the handles.

Dreamweaver resizes the AP Div to the new size.

RESIZE WITH WIDTH AND HEIGHT ATTRIBUTES

1 Click the tab in the upper-left corner of the AP Div to select it.

2 Type a new measurement into the W (width) field.

3 Press Enter (Return).

Dreamweaver changes the AP Div's width.

4 Type a new measurement into the H (height) field.

5 Press Enter (Return).

● Dreamweaver changes the AP Div's height.

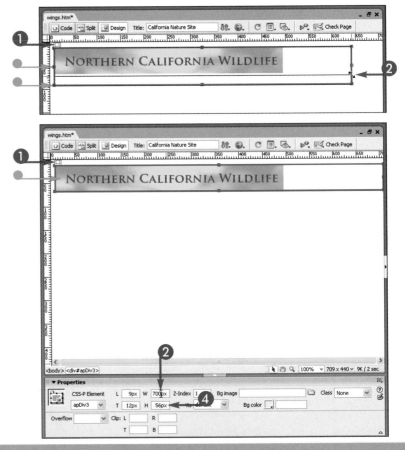

REPOSITION WITH THE CURSOR

1 Click and drag the tab in the upper-left corner of the AP Div to move it to a new position (⟨ changes to ⏉).

Dreamweaver moves the AP Div to the new location.

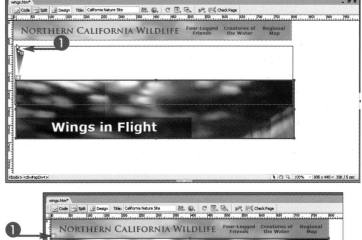

REPOSITION WITH LEFT AND TOP ATTRIBUTES

1 Click the AP Div's tab to select it.

2 Type the new distance from the left side of the window.

3 Type the new distance from the top of the window.

4 Press Enter (Return).

In this example, a 0 is entered into the Left field to position the AP Div at the far left of the page.

Dreamweaver applies the new positioning to the AP Div.

 TIPS

How can I change the visibility of an AP Div?

To change an AP Div's visibility, select an AP Div and then click the Vis ▾ in the Property inspector. You can make an AP Div visible or invisible. If it is a nested AP Div, then it can inherit its characteristics from its parent, which is the enclosing AP Div.

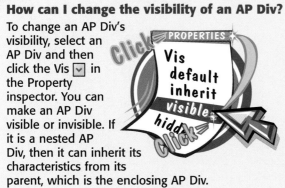

Is there any other way to tell whether an AP Div is visible or invisible?

Yes. There is a visibility column available in the AP Elements tab in the CSS panel. Click next to the AP Div name in the visibility column to adjust it. The open eye icon (👁) means that the AP Div is visible; the closed eye icon (👁) means that the AP Div is invisible. If no icon is showing, visibility is set to the default setting, and the AP Div appears visible, or inherits its visibility.

Change the Stacking Order of AP Divs

You can change the stacking order of AP Divs on a page, thus affecting how they overlap one another. You can then hide parts of some AP Divs under other AP Divs.

Change the Stacking Order of AP Divs

CHANGE ORDER IN THE AP DIVS PANEL

Note: If the CSS panel is not open, click Window and then click CSS Style to open it.

1 Click the **AP Elements** tab in the CSS panel.

2 Click and drag the AP Div name in the AP Elements panel above or below another AP Div (⟨ᴸ⟩ changes to ⏋).

Dreamweaver changes the stacking order of the AP Divs.

● If all or part of an AP Div is covered by another AP Div, it will not be visible on the page.

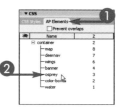

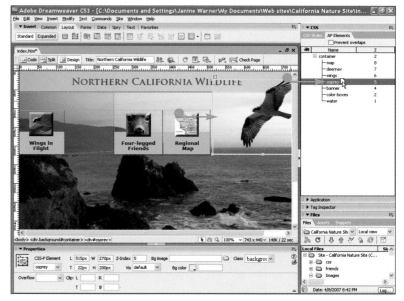

CHANGE THE ORDER WITH THE Z-INDEX ATTRIBUTE

Note: If the CSS panel is not open, click Window and then click CSS Style to open it.

1 Click the **AP Elements** tab in the CSS panel.

2 Click the name of an AP Div in the AP Elements panel to select it.

When an AP Div is selected, it becomes visible in Dreamweaver's Design area, even if it is covered by another AP Div.

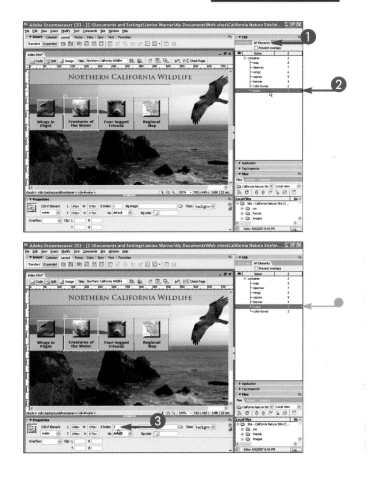

3 Type a new number in the **Z-Index** field.

The higher the Z-index of an AP Div, the higher it is placed in the stack.

● Dreamweaver changes the stacking order of the AP Divs.

TIPS

Can I use any number for the Z-index?

Yes. You can use any number for your Z-index. If you are working with many AP Divs on a page, a good technique is to number them as 10, 20, 30, and so on, instead of 1, 2, and 3. That way, if you want to position an AP Div between existing AP Divs, you can number it something like 15 or 25, and you do not have to renumber all of the other AP Divs to accommodate its new position.

How can I change the name of an AP Div?

You can change the name of an AP Div in the Property inspector. First, select the AP Div by clicking its name in the AP Elements panel or by clicking to select the AP Div in the Design area of the page. In the name field, in the top-left corner of the Property inspector, you see the current name displayed as text. Simply select the text and type the new name.

Add a Behavior to an AP Div

Using Dreamweaver behaviors with AP Divs and other elements in your pages, you can enable visitors to interact with your content, swap image files, add pop-up messages, and open new browser windows.

When you create a behavior, you select an event and an action. An *action* serves as a trigger for the behavior event.

Add a Behavior to an AP Div

Note: If the Behaviors panel is not open, click **Window** and then click **Behaviors** to open it.

1 Click to select an image or other element in your page.

In this example, a GIF image is selected from within an AP Div.

2 Click ⊞ in the Behaviors panel.

3 In the pop-up menu that appears, click **Open Browser Window**.

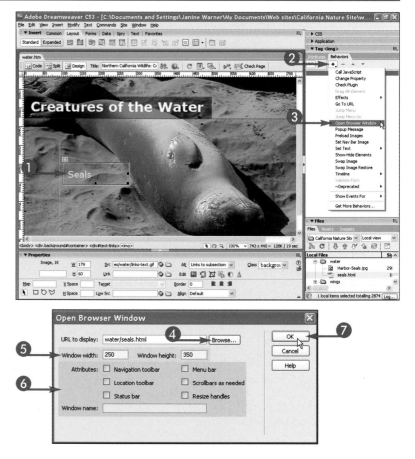

The Open Browser Window dialog box appears.

4 Click **Browse** and select a Web page that you want to open in the new browser window.

5 Type a height and width to specify the size of the browser window that will open.

6 Choose any other attributes that you want to control the browser window.

7 Click **OK**.

228

● Dreamweaver creates the behavior and displays it in the Behaviors panel.

⑧ Click here and select the **onClick** action.

In this example, onClick is selected. The result is that when a user clicks the image, a new browser window opens.

⑨ Click  to preview the page in a browser.

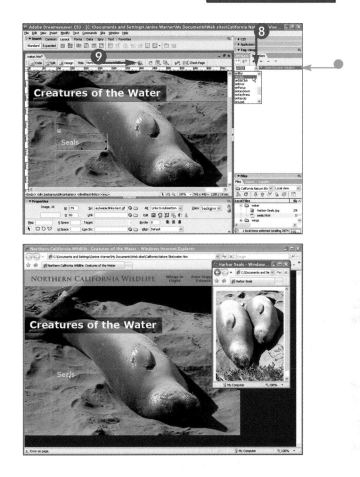

When a user clicks the image, a new browser window opens, displaying the page that you selected in the Open Browser Window dialog box.

Note: To preview a page in a Web browser, see Chapter 2.

TIPS

How do I create a rollover effect?
You can use a behavior that will be triggered when a visitor to your site rolls their cursor over an element, such as an image. To do this, select the onMouseOver option from the Behaviors panel as the trigger for the applied behavior.

Can I add behaviors?
Yes. Dreamweaver makes it easy to add new behaviors in order to add many special features to the program. Just select Get More Behaviors from the bottom of the drop-down menu in the Behaviors panel. Dreamweaver launches your default browser and takes you to the Adobe Exchange Web site where you can find many behaviors that you can download and install.

Create Complex Designs with AP Divs

You can create complex page designs using AP Divs to position elements precisely. Using drag and drop, you can move AP Divs to any place on a page.

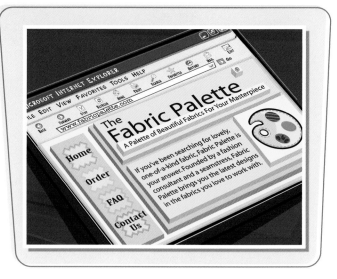

Create Complex Designs with AP Divs

● If the Layout bar is not open, click the **Layout** tab.

① Click 🖬 in the Layout Insert bar.

② Click and drag to create an AP Div.

③ Add content to the AP Div.

④ Click 🖬.

⑤ Click and drag to create a second AP Div.

⑥ Add content to the new AP Div.

You can repeat Steps **4** to **6** to create additional AP Divs with content.

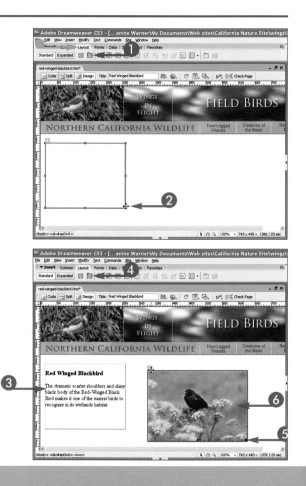

⑦ Click to select the first AP Div that you created.

⑧ In the Property inspector, type **175** in the T field.

The AP Div is now positioned 175 pixels below the top of the page.

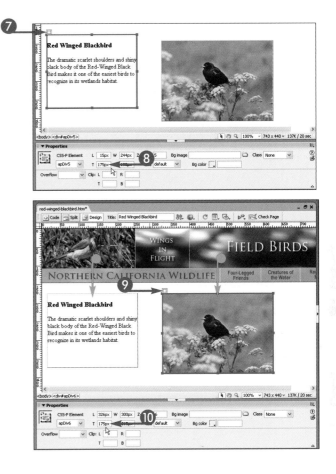

⑨ Click to select the second AP Div that you created.

⑩ In the Property inspector, type **175** in the T field.

The AP Div is now positioned 175 pixels below the top of the page, and the two AP Divs are aligned at the top.

TIPS

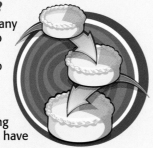

Can I add as many AP Divs as I want to a page?

Yes. You can add as many AP Divs as you want to a page, and as much content as you want to any given AP Div. You can also position the AP Divs anywhere you want on a page, moving them around until you have the design you want.

Can I place an AP Div inside another AP Div?

Yes. You can create nested AP Divs so that you can place an AP Div inside another AP Div to create an even more complex page design. For more information, see the task, "Create a Nested AP Div."

Create a Nested AP Div

A nested AP Div is often called a child AP Div, and the AP Div that contains a nested AP Div is called the parent AP Div. They act as a unit on the page; if the parent AP Div moves, the child goes with it. You can move the child AP Div independently of the parent, but the AP Divs always stay linked.

Create a Nested AP Div

Note: If the AP Elements panel is not open, click Window and then click CSS Styles to open it. Then click the AP Elements tab.

1 Click ▦.

2 Click and drag to create an AP Div.

Dreamweaver inserts an AP Div into the page.

You can insert text, images, or tables into the AP Div. In this example, text is placed in the first AP Div.

3 Click ▦.

4 Click and drag to create a new AP Div inside the first AP Div .

● Dreamweaver inserts a nested AP Div into the first AP Div.

● In the AP Elements panel, the name of the nested AP Div appears indented below the first AP Div. In this example, the AP Div, labeled *APDiv1* is nested inside an AP Div with the name *blackbird*.

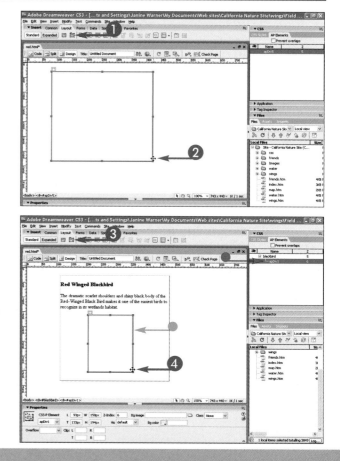

● You can insert text, images, or tables into the nested AP Div. In this example, an image is placed in the nested AP Div.

⑤ Click and drag to move the first AP Div on the page.

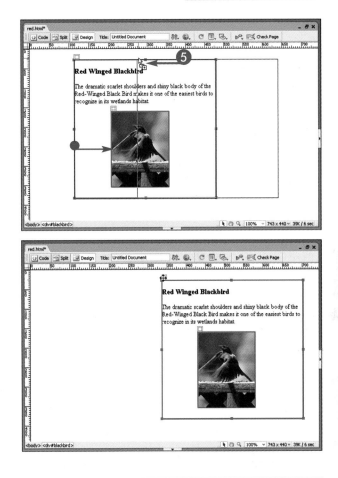

The nested, or child, AP Div moves with the parent AP Div.

Create a Centered CSS Layout

One of the limitations of AP Divs is that they cannot be centered within a browser window. To create a centered design using CSS, you have to use Divs without absolute positioning.

Dreamweaver includes many predesigned CSS Layouts from which you can choose.

Create a Centered CSS Layout

① Click **File**.

② Click **New**.

The New Document window opens.

③ Click **Blank Page**.

④ Click **HTML**.

⑤ Select a centered layout option.

⑥ Click **Create**.

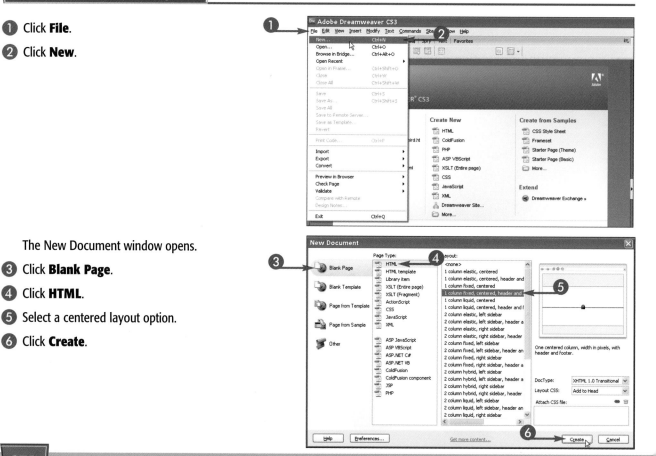

Dreamweaver creates a page with the selected layout.

7 Save the page.

8 Add a page title by changing the text here.

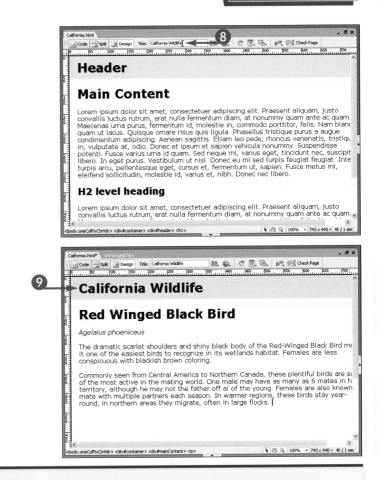

9 Replace the placeholder text in the layout with your own text.

You can also add images and other elements.

TIPS

Why can I not drag the edge of a column to change the size?

Unlike AP Divs, you cannot change a CSS layout by simply clicking and dragging. To edit the width or height of any of the Divs in a Dreamweaver CSS layout, you have to edit the CSS style. To learn more, see the task, "Edit a CSS Layout."

Can I change the background color?

Yes, you can change the background color of a CSS layout much like you would change the background color on any other page, by using the Page Properties dialog box. Click **Window** and then click **Page Properties** to open the dialog box. Choose the Background category and use the Background color field to select a color. To change the background color of an individual DIV tag in the design, you have to edit the CSS style. To learn more, see the task, "Edit a CSS Layout."

You can edit the CSS layouts that are included in Dreamweaver. However, if you are not familiar with CSS, editing one of these page layouts can be confusing.

CSS layouts cannot be edited in the Design area of Dreamweaver. You must change the styles in the CSS Styles panel to edit the layout.

Edit a CSS Layout

*Note: If the CSS Styles panel is not open, click **Window** and then click **CSS Styles** to open it.*

① Double-click the name of any style that you want to change.

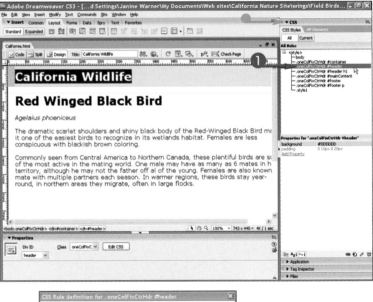

The CSS Rule Definition dialog box appears.

② Click the **Background** category.

③ Click the **Background Color Well** (👆 changes to 🖊).

④ Click a color.

⑤ Click **OK**.

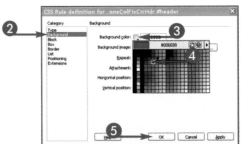

● The background color of the header changes to the selected color.

● The style updates in the CSS Styles panel, and the new style option displays in the Properties pane.

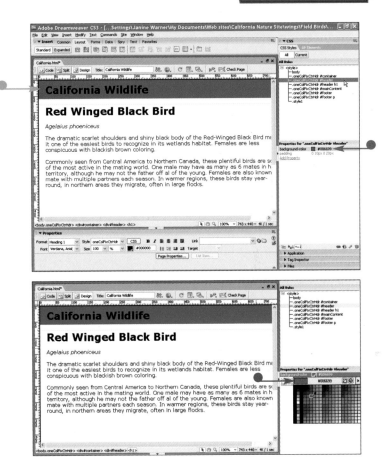

● You can also edit CSS styles in the Properties pane.

In this example, the background color is selected, displaying the color swatches.

How do I know which style corresponds to each part of the layout?

To identify what style is controlling the design of any part of the page, place your cursor in the page where you want to change the style and look at the Tag Selector at the bottom of the Design area (just above the Property inspector). In the Tag Selector, you see all of the tags that surround whatever you have selected in the Design area. Another way to identify styles is to view the HTML source code. Choose the Split view and select some text or an image that is in an area of the page that you want to edit. Then look in the code to see what style is applied to your selection.

CHAPTER 14

Publishing a Web Site

Once you are done building your Web pages, you can publish your site on a server where anyone with an Internet connection can view it. This chapter shows you how to publish your Web site and keep it up-to-date with Dreamweaver.

Publish Your Web Site

To make the Web pages that you have built in Dreamweaver accessible on the Web, you must transfer them to a Web server. A Web server is an Internet-connected computer running special software that enables the computer to serve files to Web browsers. Dreamweaver includes tools that enable you to connect and transfer pages to a Web server.

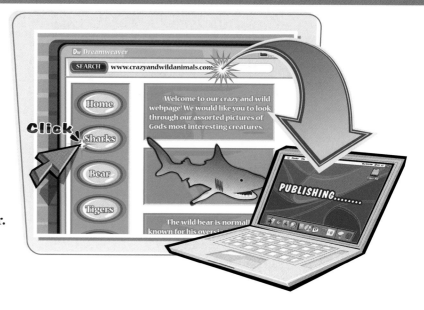

Publish Your Web Site

To publish your site files using Dreamweaver, follow these steps:

1 Specify where on your computer the site files are kept.

Note: To define a local site, see Chapter 2.

2 Specify the Web server to which you want to publish your files.

Note: To define a remote site, see the section, "Set Up a Remote Site."

Most people publish their Web pages on servers maintained by their Internet service provider (ISP), a Web-hosting company, or their company or school.

3 Connect to the Web server and transfer the files.

The Site window displays a user-friendly interface for organizing your files and transferring them to the remote site.

After uploading your site, you can update it by editing the copies of the site files on your computer (the local site) and then transferring those copies to the Web server (the remote site).

With the Site window, you can view the organization of all files in your site. You can also upload local files to the remote site and download remote files to the local site through the Files panel. You can access the Site window by clicking the Expand/Collapse button in the Files panel. For more information about the Files panel, see Chapter 3.

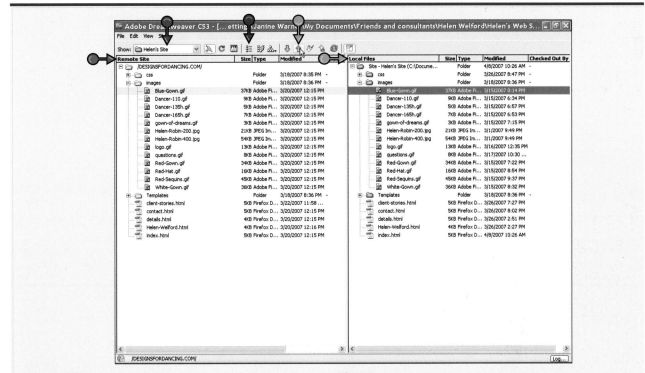

Local Files

The right pane displays the content of your site, as it exists on your local computer. To set up a local site, see Chapter 2.

Remote Site

The left pane displays the content of your site as it exists on the remote Web server. To define a remote site, see the task, "Set Up a Remote Site."

File Transfer

These buttons enable you to connect to your remote site, refresh the file list, upload files to the remote server, download files to the local site, and view the FTP log.

Site Menu

This menu allows you to select from the different sites that you have set up in Dreamweaver. For more information about setting up sites in Dreamweaver, see Chapter 2.

Site Window View

You can click ⊞ or ⬚ to switch between viewing your site as a list of files or as a site map. You can click ⬚ to access a Testing Server. For more information about using the Site Map view, see Chapter 15.

Test Your Pages in Different Browsers

There are still big differences between how HTML pages display in different browsers and different browser versions. You can preview an HTML page in any browser that is installed on your computer.

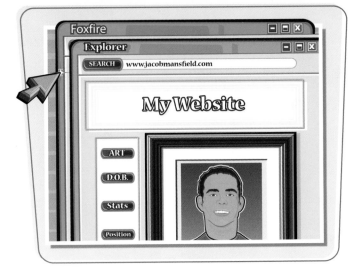

① Click **File**.

② Click **Preview in Browser**.

③ Click **Edit Browser List**.

The Preferences dialog box appears.

④ Click ⊞ in the Preview in Browser area.

The Add Browser dialog box appears.

⑤ Click **Browse**.

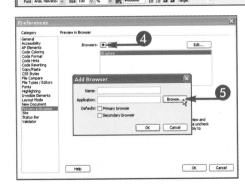

The Select Browser dialog box appears.

6 Click here and select the folder that contains a browser application.

7 Click the browser application that you want to add.

8 Click **Open**.

The Select Browser dialog box closes.

9 Click **OK** to add the browser and close the Add Browser dialog box.

10 Repeat Steps **4** to **9** to add additional browsers.

11 Click **OK** to accept your preferences and close the Preferences dialog box.

You can click ⬛ in the Document toolbar to preview an HTML page in any browser that you have added.

Where can I download older versions of browsers that are still in use?

There is a great browser archive on the Web at http://browsers.evolt.org. This nonprofit site has a comprehensive listing of current and discontinued browsers for all kinds of operating systems and versions.

What is the most popular browser?

There are dozens of browsers in use on the Web, including Netscape, Firefox, Opera, and even special browsers for the disabled that read Web pages to their users. However, the most popular browser these days, according to most sources, is Microsoft Internet Explorer.

Organize Your Files and Folders

You can use the Files panel to organize the files and folders that make up your Web site. With this panel, you can create and delete files and folders, as well as move files between folders; Dreamweaver automatically fixes any associated links.

Creating subfolders to organize files of a similar type can be useful if you have a large Web site.

Organize Your Files and Folders

① Click **Window**.

② Click **Files**.

● The Files panel displays.

③ In the Files panel, click ⊡ to display the contents of the site.

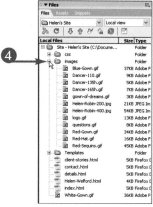

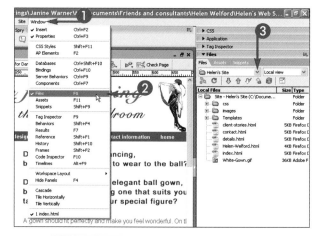

④ Click **+** to view the files in a subfolder (+ changes to –).

The folder contents display.

You can click the minus sign (**–**) to close the subfolder.

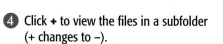

⑤ Click and drag a file from the local site folder into a subfolder (⬚ changes to ⬚).

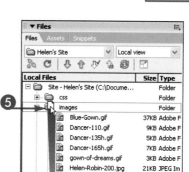

The Update Files dialog box appears, asking if you want to update your links.

⑥ Click **Update** to keep your local site links from breaking.

Dreamweaver automatically makes any changes necessary to preserve the links.

What happens to links when I move files?

When you move files into and out of folders, you need to update any hyperlinks or images that are referenced on those pages, because these references can become broken. Dreamweaver keeps track of any affected code when you rearrange files in the Files panel, and it can update the code for you when you move a file. This feature can save you time and prevent your site links from breaking.

Should I use subfolders?

Organizing your text, image, and multimedia files in subfolders can help you keep track of the contents of your Web site. Although you can store all of the files on your site in one main directory, most designers find it easier to find files when the files are organized in subfolders.

Set Up a Remote Site

The remote site is what Dreamweaver calls your site on the Web server. Think of it as a place where your Web site is made available to the rest of the world. You can set up a remote site by specifying a directory on a Web server where your site will be hosted. You can then transfer your files from your computer to the remote server.

Set Up a Remote Site

1 Click **Site**.

2 Click **Manage Sites**.

The Manage Sites dialog box appears.

3 Click a site name from the list.

4 Click **Edit**.

The Site Definition dialog box appears.

⑤ Click the **Advanced** tab.

⑥ Click **Remote Info**.

⑦ Click the Access ⬇.

⑧ Click **FTP**.

FTP is the most common way for Web designers to connect to their Web servers. The other options are only used in special situations.

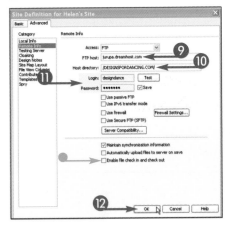

⑨ Type the name of the FTP host (Web server).

⑩ Type the directory path of your site on the Web server.

⑪ Type your login name and password.

● You can click **Enable file check in and check out** if you want to work on the site collaboratively (changes to ⬇), and enter a username and e-mail address.

⑫ Click **OK**.

The Site Definition dialog box closes.

⑬ Click **Done**.

The remote site is now set up.

 TIPS

What happens if I change my Internet service provider (ISP) and I need to move my site to a different server?

You need to change your remote site settings to enable Dreamweaver to connect to your new ISP server. Your local site settings can stay the same. Make sure that you keep your local files current and backed up before you change servers.

How do I register a domain name?

You can register a domain name at a number of domain registration services on the Internet. Two of the most popular, and least expensive, are www.godaddy.com and www.1and1.com. As long as you pay the annual fee (less than $10 a year at these sites), the domain is yours. To direct the domain to your Web site, you need to specify where your Web server is at the domain registration service.

reservations:
WWW.GODADDY OR
WWW.1AND1.COM

Connect to a Remote Site

You can connect to the Web server that hosts your remote site and transfer files between it and Dreamweaver. Dreamweaver connects to the Web server by a process known as File Transfer Protocol, or FTP.

Before you can connect to a remote server, you need to set up your remote site. For more information, see the task, "Set Up a Remote Site."

① In the Files panel, click **Expand Site Panel** (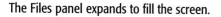) to expand the remote and local site panels.

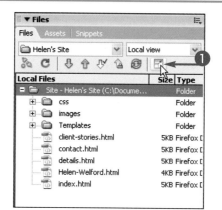

The Files panel expands to fill the screen.

② Click **Connect** (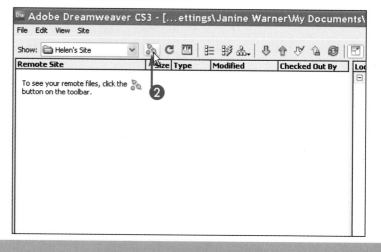) to connect to the Web server.

Note: Dreamweaver displays an alert dialog box if it cannot connect to the site. If you have trouble connecting, then review the host information that you entered for the remote site.

● When you are connected to the Internet, 🔌 changes to 🔌.

Dreamweaver displays the contents of the remote site's host directory.

③ Click **+** to view the contents of a directory on the Web server (+ changes to −).

Dreamweaver displays the contents of the directory.

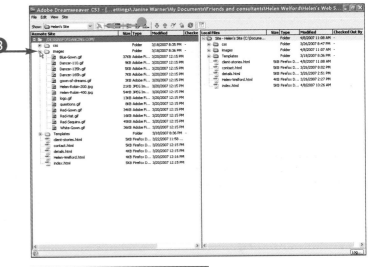

④ Click **Disconnect** (🔌).

Dreamweaver disconnects from the Web server.

If you do not transfer any files for 30 minutes, Dreamweaver automatically disconnects from a Web server.

TIPS

How do I keep Dreamweaver from prematurely disconnecting from the Web server?

You can click **Edit**, then click **Preferences**, and then click **Site**. You can adjust the FTP transfer options to change the time that Dreamweaver allows to pass between commands before it logs you off the server — the default is 30 minutes. Note that Web servers also have a similar setting on their end. Therefore, the server, not Dreamweaver, may sometimes log you off if you are inactive for more than the server's allotted time.

What if the connection does not work?

If Dreamweaver fails to connect to your server, then your Internet connection may be down. Make sure your computer is connected to the Internet and try again. If you still cannot connect, then you may have incorrectly entered the FTP settings. Check with your service provider or system Administrator if you are not sure about your Web server settings.

Upload Files to a Web Server

You can use Dreamweaver's FTP features to upload files from your local site to your remote server, to make your Web pages available to others on the Internet.

PUBLISH FILES ONLINE

① Click ⬛ to connect to the Web server through the Site window (⬛ changes to ⬛).

② Click the file or folder that you want to upload.

③ Click **Put** (⬆).

You can also right-click the file and select **Put** from the menu that appears.

A dialog box appears, asking if you want to include dependent files.

Dependent files are images and other files associated with a particular page. If you are uploading a page that displays images, then those images are dependent files.

④ Click **Yes** or **No**.

● You can click here (☐ changes to ☑) to avoid seeing this dialog box again.

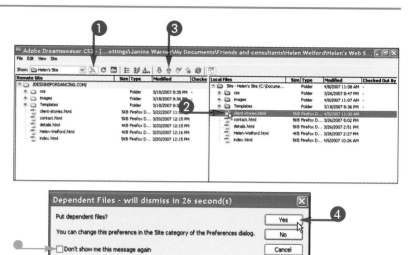

● The file transfers from your computer to the Web, and the filename appears in the Remote files panel.

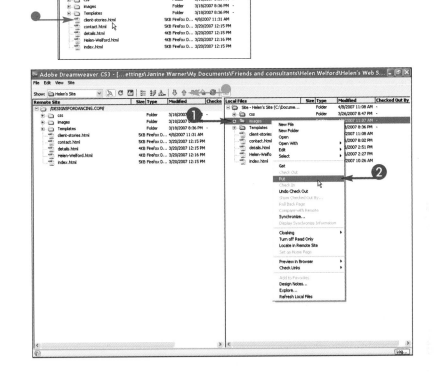

UPLOAD A FOLDER

① In the right pane, right-click the folder that you want to upload.

② Click **Put** in the menu that appears.

● You can also click 🖿 and then click 🔼.

Dreamweaver transfers the folder and its contents from your computer to the Web server.

How do I stop a file transfer in progress?

You can click Cancel from the Status window that appears while a transfer is in progress. You can also press Esc to cancel a file transfer.

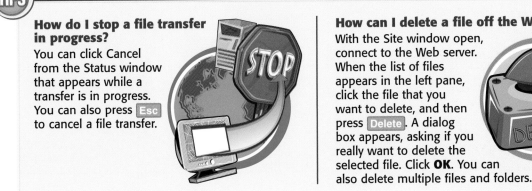

How can I delete a file off the Web server?

With the Site window open, connect to the Web server. When the list of files appears in the left pane, click the file that you want to delete, and then press Delete. A dialog box appears, asking if you really want to delete the selected file. Click **OK**. You can also delete multiple files and folders.

Download Files from a Web Server

You can download files from your remote site in Dreamweaver if you need to retrieve them. Once they are downloaded, you can make changes or updates to the pages in Dreamweaver and then put them back on the Web server.

Download Files from a Web Server

DOWNLOAD FILES

① Click 🔧 to connect to the Web server (🔧 changes to 🔧).

② Click the file that you want to download.

③ Click **Get** (⬇).

You can also right-click the file in the remote site and select **Get** in the menu that appears.

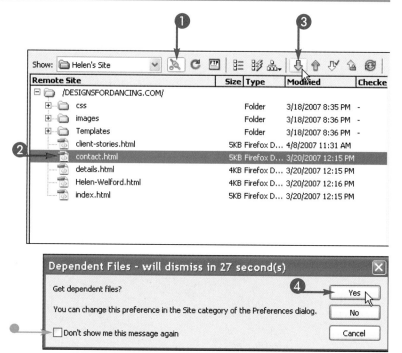

A dialog box appears, asking if you want to include dependent files.

Dependent files are images and other files associated with a particular page. If you are downloading a page that displays images, then those images are dependent files.

④ Click **Yes** or **No**.

● You can click the check box (☐ changes to ☑) to avoid seeing this dialog box again.

● The file transfers from the Web server to your computer.

If the file already exists on your local computer, then a dialog box appears, asking whether it is okay to overwrite it.

Local Files	Size	Type	Modified	Checked Out By
☐ 🗀 Site - Helen's Site (C:\Docume...		Folder	4/8/2007 11:08 AM	-
⊞ 🗀 css		Folder	3/26/2007 8:47 PM	-
⊞ 🗀 images		Folder	4/8/2007 11:07 AM	-
⊞ 🗀 Templates		Folder	3/18/2007 8:36 PM	-
client-stories.html	5KB	Firefox D...	4/8/2007 11:08 AM	
contact.html	5KB	Firefox D...	3/26/2007 8:02 PM	
details.html	5KB	Firefox D...	3/26/2007 2:51 PM	
Helen-Welford.html	4KB	Firefox D...	3/26/2007 2:27 PM	
index.html	5KB	Firefox D...	4/8/2007 10:26 AM	

DOWNLOAD MULTIPLE FILES

1 Press and hold Ctrl (Control) and click to select the files that you want to download.

2 Click 🔽.

The files transfer from your Web server to your computer.

The downloaded files appear in the Local Files panel.

Show: 🗀 Helen's Site

Remote Site	Size	Type	Modified	Checke
☐ 🗀 /DESIGNSFORDANCING.COM/				
⊞ 🗀 css		Folder	3/18/2007 8:35 PM	-
⊞ 🗀 images		Folder	3/18/2007 8:36 PM	-
⊞ 🗀 Templates		Folder	3/18/2007 8:36 PM	-
client-stories.html	5KB	Firefox D...	4/8/2007 11:31 AM	
contact.html	5KB	Firefox D...	3/20/2007 12:15 PM	
details.html	4KB	Firefox D...	3/20/2007 12:15 PM	
Helen-Welford.html	4KB	Firefox D...	3/20/2007 12:16 PM	
index.html	5KB	Firefox D...	3/20/2007 12:15 PM	

TIPS

Where does Dreamweaver log errors that occur during file transfer?

Dreamweaver logs all transfer activity, including errors, in a file-transfer log. You can view it by clicking **Window**, then clicking **Results**, and then clicking **FTP Log**. The FTP Log panel appears at the bottom of the screen.

Can I use my Web site to store files while I am still working on them?

If a file is on your Web server, then it can be viewed on the Internet. When pages are under construction and you do not want them to be seen, you should not put them up on your Web site, even temporarily. Even if the page is not linked to your site, someone may find it, or a search engine may even index and cache it.

Synchronize Your Local and Remote Sites

Dreamweaver can synchronize files between your local and remote sites so that both sites have an identical set of the most recent files. This can be useful if other people are editing the files on the remote site, and you need to update your local copies of those files. It is also handy if you edit pages and you do not remember all of the pages that you need to upload.

Synchronize Your Local and Remote Sites

1 Click ⚙ to connect to the Web server (⚙ changes to ⚙).

2 Click Synchronize (⊚).

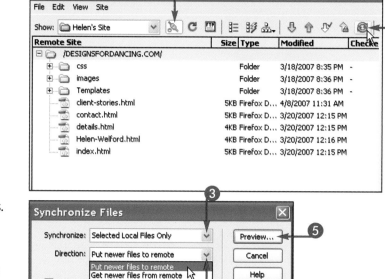

The Synchronize Files dialog box appears.

3 Click here and select the files that you want to synchronize.

4 Click here and select a direction in which you want to copy the files.

You can place the newest copies on both the remote and local sites by selecting **Get and Put newer files**.

5 Click **Preview**.

Dreamweaver compares the sites and then lists the files for transfer, based on your selections in Steps **3** and **4**.

6 Click to select the files that you do not want to transfer.

7 With the files selected, click **Trash** (🗑) to remove them from the transfer list.

8 Click **OK**.

● Dreamweaver transfers the files.

The local and remote sites are now synchronized.

Are there other FTP tools besides those available from Dreamweaver?

Dreamweaver offers the convenience of transferring files without having to open other programs. However, the application uses many system resources and can significantly slow down some computers. There are many good alternatives available. For example, in Windows, you can use WS_FTP. In Mac OS, you can use Transmit or Fetch. You can download evaluation copies of these programs from www.download.com. Other alternatives for transferring files through FTP include CuteFTP, LeechFTP, and CoffeeCup Direct FTP.

Today's
FTP Specials
• WS_FTP
• CuteFTP
• Fetch

Maintaining a Web Site

Maintaining a Web site and keeping its content fresh can be as much work as creating the site. Dreamweaver's site-maintenance tools make updating faster and easier.

View the Site Map

The Site Map view enables you to view your site as a flowchart with lines representing links that connect the document icons. This view also helps you to maintain your site by highlighting broken internal links.

The Dreamweaver Site Map feature should not be confused with site maps that often appear on Web sites. This feature is for organizational use, and is not to be published on your Web site.

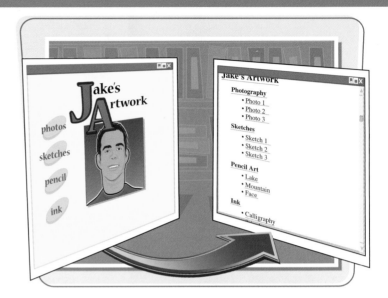

View the Site Map

Note: You must first set up a site before you can use the Site Map feature. To set up a site using the Files window, see Chapter 2.

① In the Files panel, click ☑.

② Click **Map view**.

A site map appears in the Files panel. By default, the site map displays the site structure two levels deep, beginning from the home page.

③ In the Files panel, click **Expand Site Panel** (☐) to expand the map display.

● You can also click and drag the side of the Files panel to expand it (☼ changes to ↘).

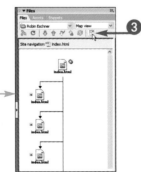

The site map fills the screen.

④ Click .

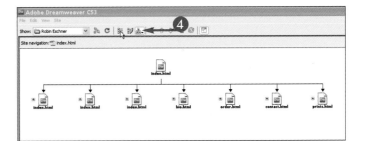

The Local Files panel displays on the right side of the screen.

● To view files below the second level, you can click +.

● External links are marked with an External Link icon (📄).

● To close the Expanded view, you can click 📄.

To save the site map as a BMP image that you can print or view in an image editor, click **File** and then click **Save Site Map**.

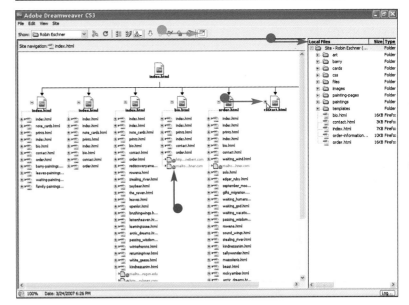

TIPS

How do I fix a broken link in the site map?

A broken chain icon in the site map means that the link to a page is broken. You can fix a broken link by right-clicking (Option -clicking) the destination page and then clicking **Change Link** from the menu that appears. Links can break because a destination page is renamed or deleted.

How can I make changes to the layout of the site map?

From the site window, click **View** and then click **Layout**. The Site Definition window appears, displaying the Site Map Layout options. You can select the home page, specify the number of columns and rows to display, specify whether to identify files by their names or titles, and choose whether to view hidden and dependent files.

Manage
Site Assets

You can view and manage elements that appear in the pages of your site with the Assets panel. The Assets panel provides an easy way to insert elements that you want to use more than once in your site.

① Click **Window**.

② Click **Assets**.

● You can also click the **Assets** tab in the Files panel to open the Assets panel.

The Assets panel appears, displaying objects from the selected category.

③ Click the name of any asset to preview it in the Assets panel.

● Click and drag the side of the Assets panel to expand it.

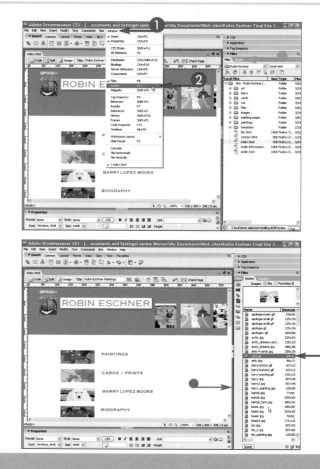

The Assets panel displays in the new dimensions, and previews your selected asset.

④ Click a column heading.

The assets are now sorted under the selected column heading in descending order. You can click the column again to sort in ascending order.

To view other assets, you can click a different category button.

TIP

How are assets organized?
Items in the Assets panel are organized into the following categories:

	Images	GIF, JPG, and PNG images
	Color	Text, background, link, and style-sheet colors
	URLs	Accessible external Web addresses
	Flash	Flash-based multimedia
	Shockwave	Shockwave-based multimedia
	Movie	QuickTime and MPEG movies
	Scripts	External JavaScript or VBScript files
	Templates	Page-layout templates
	Library	Library of reusable page elements

Add Content with the Assets Panel

You can add frequently used content to your site directly from the Assets panel. This technique can be more efficient than using a menu command or the Insert panel.

Add Content with the Assets Panel

INSERT AN IMAGE OR FILE

① Click inside the Document window where you want to insert the asset.

② Click the **Assets** tab to open the Assets panel.

③ Click a category.

④ Click an asset.

⑤ Drag the asset onto the page.

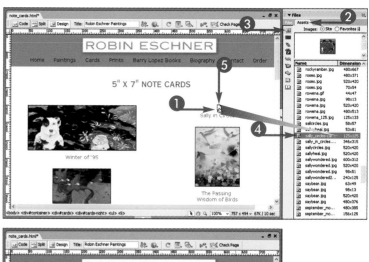

Dreamweaver inserts the asset into your Document window.

In this example, an image is added to the page.

You can also click the Insert button at the bottom of the Assets panel.

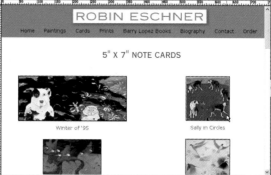

EDIT CONTENT USING THE ASSETS PANEL

① Click the object to which you want to apply the asset in the Document window.

② Click a category.

This example uses Colors (▦).

③ Click an asset.

④ Click **Apply**.

You can also drag and drop the asset from the Assets panel onto the selected object in the Document window.

Dreamweaver applies the asset in the Document window.

In this example, color is applied to the text.

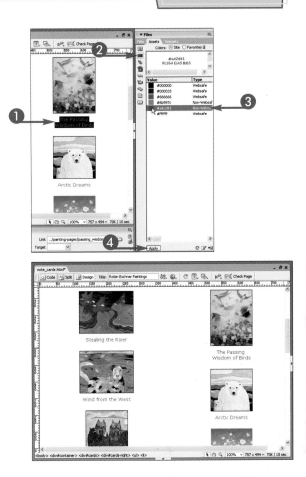

How do I copy assets from one site to another?

Click one or more items in the Assets panel, and then right-click (Option-click) the selected assets. From the menu that appears, click **Copy to Site** and then click a site to which you want to copy the assets. The assets appear in the Favorites list under the same category in the other site.

Are all of my links saved in the Assets panel?

Only links to external Web sites and e-mail addresses are saved in the Assets panel. Links to internal pages in your site are not saved in the Assets panel. You can use the saved links in the Assets panel to quickly create new links to Web sites and e-mail addresses to which you have already linked in your site.

Specify Favorite Assets

To make your asset lists more manageable, you can organize assets that you use often into a Favorites list inside each asset category.

GATHER FAVORITE ASSETS

1. Click the **Assets** tab to open the Assets panel.

2. Click a category.

3. Click an asset.

4. Right-click (Option-click) the selected asset and click **Add to Favorites** from the menu that appears.

● You can also click 📷.

   Dreamweaver adds the asset to the category Favorites list.

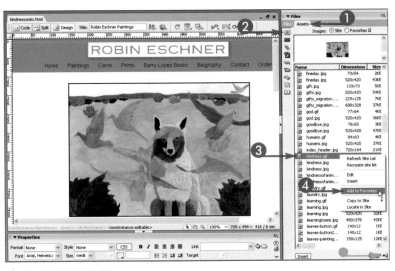

5. Click **Favorites** (○ changes to ◉).

● The selected asset appears in the Favorites category.

NICKNAME A FAVORITE ASSET

1 Click a category.

2 Click **Favorites** (○ changes to ◉).

You cannot nickname regular assets.

3 Right-click (Option-click) an asset.

4 Click **Edit Nickname** from the menu that appears.

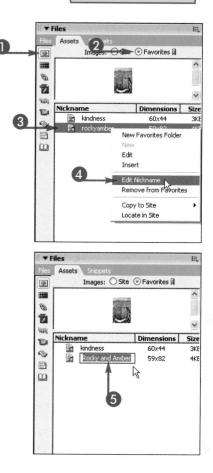

5 Type a nickname.

6 Press Enter (Return).

The nickname appears in the Favorites list.

How do I remove an item entirely from the Assets panel?

You need to delete the item from your local site folder. You can right-click (Option-click) the item in the Files panel, then click **Edit**, and then click **Delete** from the menu that appears. When you return to the Assets panel and click the **Refresh** button, the asset is gone. You can also delete an item from the Site panel by clicking 📃 in the Files panel and then following the same steps described above.

How do I add items to the Assets panel?

You do not need to add items. One of the handiest things about the Assets panel is that every time you add an image, external link, e-mail link, color, or multimedia asset to your Web site, Dreamweaver automatically stores it in the Assets panel.

Check a Page In or Out

Dreamweaver provides a Check in/Check out system that keeps track of files when a team is working on a Web site. For example, when one person checks out a page from the Web server, others cannot access the same file.

When the Check in/Check out system is off, multiple people can edit the same file at once.

Check a Page In or Out

ENABLE CHECK IN/CHECK OUT

Note: You first need to specify the remote settings, and connect to your remote Web server to use the Check in/Check out function. To set up a remote site and connect to it, see Chapter 14.

① Click **Site**.

② Click **Manage Sites**.

The Manage Sites dialog box appears.

③ Click to select the name of a site.

④ Click **Edit**.

The Site Definition dialog box appears.

⑤ Click the **Advanced** tab.

⑥ Click **Remote Info**.

⑦ Click **Enable file check in and check out** (□ changes to ☑).

⑧ Type your name and e-mail address.

⑨ Click **OK** to accept your changes.

⑩ Click **Done** in the Manage Sites dialog box.

Check in/Check out is now enabled.

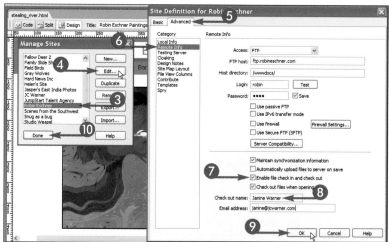

CHECK OUT A FILE

1. Click to select a file in the Files panel that is not checked out, and then right-click (Option-click) it.

2. Click **Check Out**.

   Dreamweaver marks the page as checked out.

CHECK IN A FILE

1. Click to select a file that you have checked out, and then right-click (Option-click) it.

2. Click **Check In**.

   Dreamweaver marks the page as checked in.

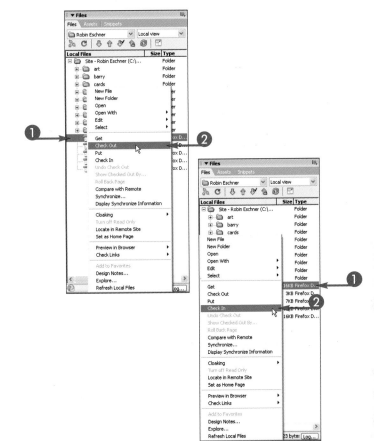

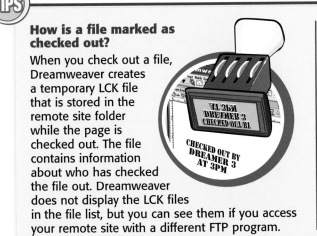

How is a file marked as checked out?

When you check out a file, Dreamweaver creates a temporary LCK file that is stored in the remote site folder while the page is checked out. The file contains information about who has checked the file out. Dreamweaver does not display the LCK files in the file list, but you can see them if you access your remote site with a different FTP program.

Can I e-mail someone who has a file checked out to tell them that I need it?

Yes. Dreamweaver collects usernames and e-mail addresses in the Check in and Check out fields to make it easy for multiple people who are working on the same Web site to stay in touch. If someone else has a file checked out, you can use the Check in/Check out feature to send them an e-mail message.

Make Design Notes

If you are working on a site collaboratively, Design Notes enable you to add information about the development status of a file. For example, you can attach information to your Web pages, such as editing history and an author name.

Make Design Notes

① Open the Web page to which you want to attach a Design Note.

② Click **File**.

③ Click **Design Notes**.

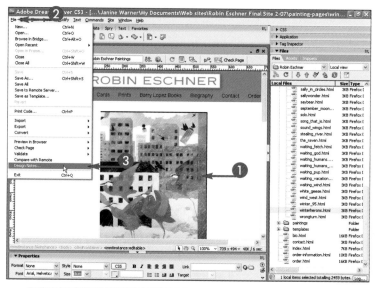

The Design Notes dialog box appears.

④ Click here and select a status for the page.

⑤ Type a note.

⑥ Click **Date** (📅) to enter the current date in the Notes field.

● You can click **Show when file is opened** (☐ changes to ☑) to automatically show Design Notes when a file opens.

⑦ Click the **All info** tab.

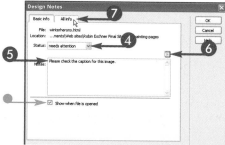

The All info tab displays.

8 To enter new information into Design Notes, click ⊞.

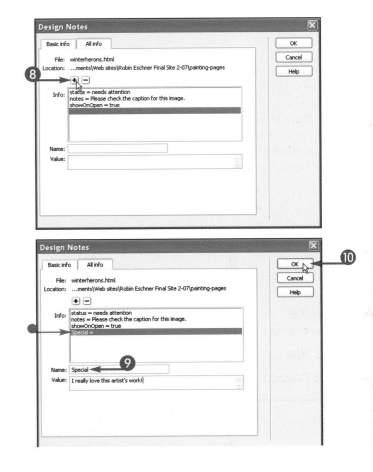

9 Type a name and associated value.

● The added value pair appears in the Info section.

You can delete information by clicking it in the Info section and then clicking ⊟.

10 Click **OK**.

Dreamweaver makes the Design Note.

How can I view Design Notes?

You can view Design Notes in two ways. First, files with a Design Note have a yellow bubble in the site window. Double-click it to open the Design Note. Alternatively, you can open any file with an attached Design Note, then click **File**, and then click **Design Notes** to open the Design Note.

Are Design Notes private?

Although Design Notes are not linked to the page or displayed in a Web browser, anyone with access to your server can view your Design Notes. If someone is especially clever and your server does not protect the notes folder, then they may find it, even without password access to your site. Ultimately, Design Notes are useful for communication among Web designers, but they are not meant to protect important secrets.

Run a Site Report

Running a site report can help you pinpoint problems in your site, including redundant HTML code in your pages and missing page titles. It is a good idea to test your site by running a report before you upload it to a Web server.

① Click **Site**.

② Click **Reports**.

The Reports dialog box appears.

③ Click here and select to run a report on either the entire site or selected files.

④ Click the reports that you want to run (☐ changes to ☑).

⑤ Click **Run**.

Dreamweaver creates a report and displays it in the Results panel of the Property inspector.

⑥ Click any tab across the top of the Results panel to display the report.

You can search and replace all of the hyperlinks on your site that point to a specific address. This is helpful when a page is renamed or deleted and the links to it need to be updated.

Change a Link Sitewide

① Click **Site**.

② Click **Change Link Sitewide**.

The Change Link Sitewide dialog box appears.

③ Type the old hyperlink destination that you want to change.

④ Type the new hyperlink destination.

The hyperlinks must start with a forward slash (/), and be a `mailto:` (e-mail) link, or a full URL.

⑤ Click **OK**.

Dreamweaver finds and replaces all instances of the old destination. A dialog box asks you to confirm the changes.

Find and Replace Text

The Find and Replace feature is a powerful tool for making changes to text elements that repeat across many pages. You can find and replace text on your Web page, your source code, or specific HTML tags in your pages.

① Click **Edit**.

② Click **Find and Replace**.

The Find and Replace dialog box appears.

③ Click here and select whether you want to search the entire site or only selected files.

④ Click here and select the type of text that you want to search.

For example, you can select **Text (Advanced)** to find text that is inside a specific tag.

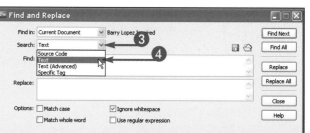

⑤ Type the text that you want to find.

● You can click **Find Next** to find instances of your query one at a time.

⑥ Type the replacement text.

⑦ Click **Replace** to replace the text instances one at a time.

● You can also click **Replace All** to automatically replace all instances of your text search.

If Dreamweaver asks whether you want to replace text in unopened documents, you can click **Yes**.

● Dreamweaver replaces the text, and the details appear in the bottom of the screen in the Results panel.

Find and Replace

Find in: Current Document — Barry Lopez Inspired — Find Next

Search: Text — Find All

Find: artist ⑤ — Replace ⑦

Replace: painter ⑥ — Replace All

Options: ☑ Match case — ☑ Ignore whitespace — Close

☑ Match whole word — ☐ Use regular expression — Help

▼ **Results** Search | Reference | Validation | Browser Compatibility Check | Link Checker | Site Reports | FTP Log | Server Debug

File — Matched Text

● [current document] — Robin Eschner is a _painter_ and composer living in Northern California.

Done. 1 item found. 1 replaced in the current document.

TIPS

Can I use the Find and Replace feature to alter HTML code?

Yes. Searching for a string of code is a quick way to make changes to a Web site. For example, if you want to alter the body color for every page, then you can search for the HTML <body> tag and replace it with a different color tag.

Can I use the Find and Replace feature to alter an HTML attribute?

Yes. You can replace attributes to achieve many things. For example, you can change the alignment of the contents of a table (change align="center" to align="right" in <td> tags); change the color of specific text in your page (change color="green" to color="red" in <font> tags); or change the page background color across your site (change bgcolor= "black" to bgcolor="white" in <body> tags).

Building a Database-Driven Web Site

If you are an advanced Dreamweaver user who understands databases, then you can read this chapter to learn how to use server behaviors to create powerful and dynamic Web sites.

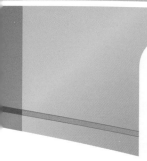

The Power of Dynamic Web Sites

Some of the most advanced Web sites are created by combining the power of a database with technology that delivers Web pages dynamically. Many of the Web sites that you visit for news, weather, e-mail, forums, and shopping are created using databases and dynamic Web technologies.

Database-Driven Web Sites

Dynamic Web pages communicate with a database, XML file, or other content source to display and store content on demand. You can store thousands of pages of information and images in a database. You can then create a handful of dynamic Web pages that allow you to browse or search that content. This is much more efficient than creating a thousand individual HTML pages!

Growth- and Maintenance-Friendly

Dynamic Web sites are built to handle ever-changing content. For example, e-commerce sites typically consist of a few carefully designed templates that are used to display the contents of the database. Storing data in a database can make it easier to update because when the same data appears on multiple pages in your Web site, you only need to update it once in the database. A database is also more adaptable — you can sort, find, delete, and add information faster in a database than by manually browsing through individual Web pages.

Involve Your Users

Databases are not just about storing content; they can also collect and share data on demand. Web sites such as eBay, Yahoo!, and Amazon.com are powered by complex databases. Dynamic Web sites such as these enable you to display and receive information from anyone who participates in dynamic areas of the sites. For example, the ability to store user information in a database enables Amazon.com to recommend books based on your previous purchases.

Install a Testing Server

A Testing Server, also called an Application Server, is software that enables a computer to receive connections from Web browsers. This software supports technologies such as ASP, PHP, and ColdFusion, which act as the liaison between your database and your Web pages.

This section assumes that you are running Windows XP Professional. You may need your Windows XP installation disc to install IIS. If IIS is not available for your version of Windows, then you can download Personal Web Server from www.microsoft.com.

Install a Testing Server

① Click **Start**.

② Click **Control Panel**.

③ In the Control Panel that appears, click **Add or Remove Programs**.

The Add or Remove Programs window appears.

④ Click **Add/Remove Windows Components**.

● If you are using Windows XP, the Windows XP Setup window appears while setup takes place.

The Windows Components Wizard appears.

⑤ Click **Internet Information Services (IIS)**
(☐ changes to ☑).

If Internet Information Services (IIS) is already
checked, you can click **Cancel** and skip to Step 15.

⑥ Click **Next**.

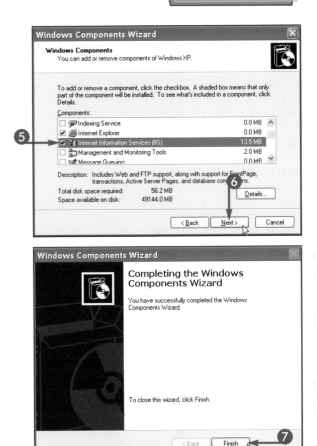

A progress screen lets you know how the
installation is going.

Note: *You may receive a prompt asking you to insert your Windows
Installation CD-ROM into the CD-ROM drive. If you receive this prompt,
then complete this step.*

The Windows Component Wizard completion
page appears.

⑦ Click **Finish**.

Why does Windows need the installation CD-ROM?
Windows is made up of thousands of individual files and
programs. In order to save space on your computer's hard
drive, Windows copies only the files that it needs when
you originally install it. When you install a Windows
component, such as Internet Information Services,
Windows sometimes needs to copy these files from the
CD-ROM and put them on your computer's hard drive.

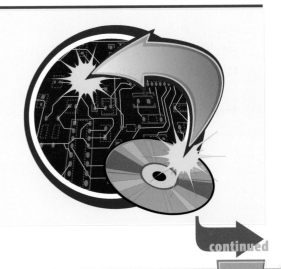

continued

Windows XP Professional ships with Internet Information Server (IIS). IIS is an application server that processes Active Server Pages (ASP) and makes it easy for you to create dynamic pages.

Install a Testing Server *(continued)*

⑧ Click **Start**.

⑨ Click **All Programs**.

⑩ Click **Administrative Tools**.

⑪ Click **Internet Information Services**.

The Internet Information Services window appears.

⑫ Right-click **Default Web Site** (🖳).

⑬ Click **Properties**.

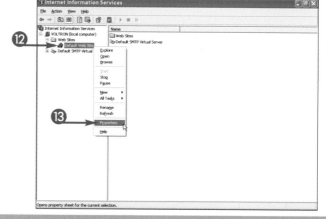

The Default Web Site Properties dialog box appears.

Note: IIS allows you to control various Web site settings, such as public folder browsing. For more information on IIS, visit www.microsoft.com.

14 Click **OK** to close the window.

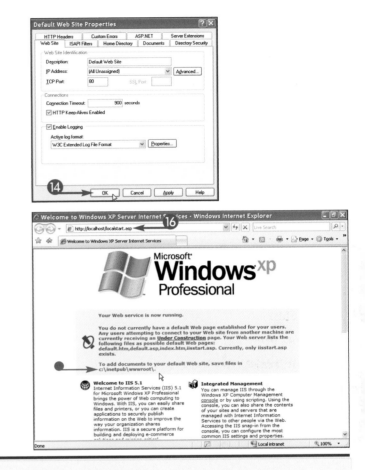

15 Open your Web browser.

16 Type **http://localhost/**.

The default Testing Server page displays, telling you that the server was installed correctly.

● This page also tells you where to move your Web site. The path is usually at c:\inetpub\wwwroot\.

TIP

What should I do if I cannot find the Administrative Tools folder?

Windows does not automatically show the Administrative Tools folder. To show the folder:

1 Right-click **Start**.

2 Click **Properties**.

3 Click **Customize**.

4 Click the **Advanced** tab.

5 Click the **Display on the All Programs menu** option (○ changes to ⦿).

6 Click **OK**.

7 Click **OK**.

Create a Database Connection

A data source name, or DSN, is used to store database connection settings. Acting as a bookmark, it allows you to conveniently connect to your database from applications without defining the settings for the database every time. You must first create a database before defining a DSN.

This example uses a simple database that was created with Microsoft Access 2000, a popular database program for Windows.

Create a Database Connection

① Click **Start**.

② Click **All Programs**.

③ Click **Administrative Tools**.

④ Click **Data Sources (ODBC)**.

Windows XP hides folders that you do not regularly use. Click the double-arrow down to expand hidden items if the Data Sources option is not visible.

The ODBC Data Source Administrator dialog box appears.

⑤ Click the **System DSN** tab.

⑥ Click **Add**.

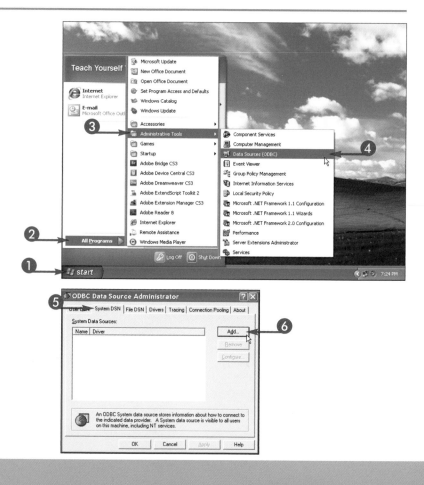

The Create New Data Source dialog box appears with a list of database drivers.

7 Click **Microsoft Access Driver [*mdb]**.

8 Click **Finish**.

The ODBC Microsoft Access Setup dialog box appears.

9 Type a unique, descriptive name for your database.

10 Click **Select**.

continued

TIPS

What is a server-side programming language? Is HTML a server-side programming language?

HTML is a markup language, meaning that its primary use is to display content. However, it was developed to connect with other technologies. Server-side programming languages such as ASP, PHP, JSP, and ColdFusion are languages that are used to create programs that reside on a server and make database communication possible. Dreamweaver CS3 server behaviors write server-side programming code for you.

What is the difference between a system DSN, a user DSN, and a file DSN?

All three DSN types store the same kind of database connectivity information. You use a system DSN when you want every user on the computer to have access to the database. A user DSN only allows specific computer users to access the database, usually the user who creates it. Both system and user DSNs store the information inside the registry. A file DSN creates a DSN file, storing the information inside this text file instead of in the registry.

If your application server is running on a Windows system, then you can use a DSN to connect your dynamic Web pages to a database.

Create a Database Connection *(continued)*

The Select Database dialog box appears.

⑪ Click here and select the drive where the database is located.

⑫ Click the folder in which the database is located.

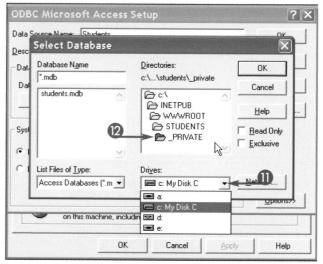

⑬ Click the desired MDB file (Microsoft Access Database file).

⑭ Click **OK**.

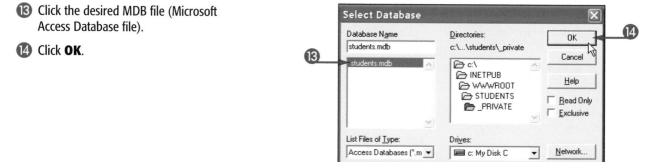

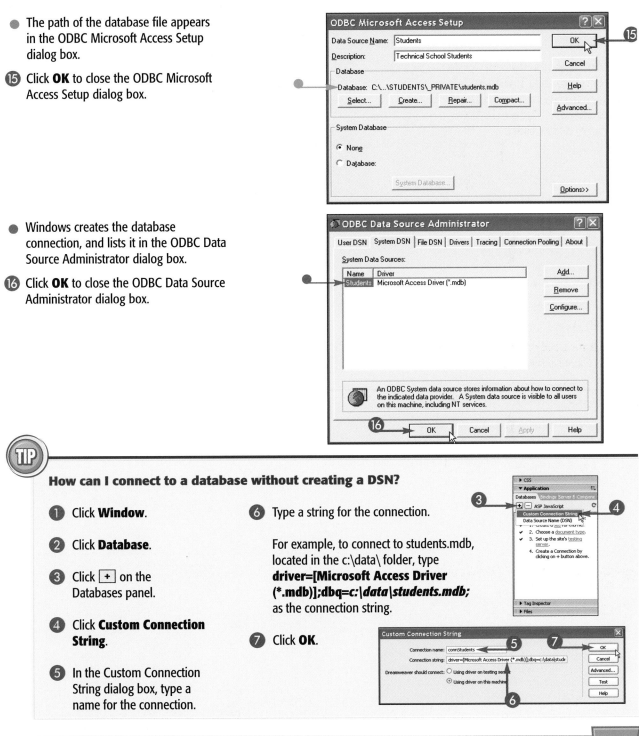

- The path of the database file appears in the ODBC Microsoft Access Setup dialog box.

⓯ Click **OK** to close the ODBC Microsoft Access Setup dialog box.

- Windows creates the database connection, and lists it in the ODBC Data Source Administrator dialog box.

⓰ Click **OK** to close the ODBC Data Source Administrator dialog box.

TIP

How can I connect to a database without creating a DSN?

① Click **Window**.

② Click **Database**.

③ Click ➕ on the Databases panel.

④ Click **Custom Connection String**.

⑤ In the Custom Connection String dialog box, type a name for the connection.

⑥ Type a string for the connection.

For example, to connect to students.mdb, located in the c:\data\ folder, type **driver=[Microsoft Access Driver (*.mdb)];dbq=*c:\data\students.mdb;*** as the connection string.

⑦ Click **OK**.

Configure a Dynamic Web Site

Dynamic Web pages do not display database content when you open them directly from a Web browser. As a result, you must configure Dreamweaver to use your Testing Server. These features create a seamless authoring environment for you.

Configure a Dynamic Web Site

ASSOCIATE THE TESTING SERVER

1 Click **Site**.

2 Click **Manage Sites**.

The Manage Sites dialog box appears.

3 Click a site.

4 Click **Edit**.

Note: You must either move all of the contents of your site into your Testing Server area (usually a folder inside c:\inetpub\wwwroot), or configure IIS to point to its current folder. For more information about the Testing Server, see the task, "Install a Testing Server."

The Site Definition dialog box appears.

5 Click the **Advanced** tab.

6 Click **Testing Server**.

7 Click here and select **ASP VBScript**.

8 Click here and select **Local/Network**.

9 Click here and select where your site is located on your computer.

10 Type the path to your local site folder, starting with the URL prefix **http://localhost/**.

11 Click **OK**.

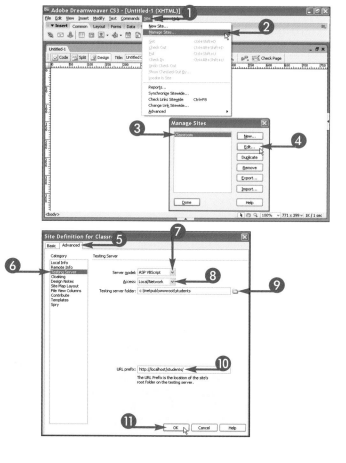

ASSOCIATE AND TEST YOUR CONNECTION

① Click the Application panel to see the checklist of items that are necessary to test your connection.

② Click any unchecked links.

Note: *If the Testing Server option is not checked, then you must verify that one is associated with your site, and ensure that IIS is running properly.*

③ Click ⊞ and select **Data Source Name (DSN)**.

The Data Source Name (DSN) dialog box appears.

④ Type a connection name.

⑤ Click here and select your DSN.

To create, edit, or troubleshoot your connections, you can click **Define**.

⑥ Click **Test**.

A dialog box appears, confirming your connection.

⑦ Click **OK**.

A 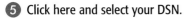 appears in your database panel, representing a working connection.

⑧ Click **OK**.

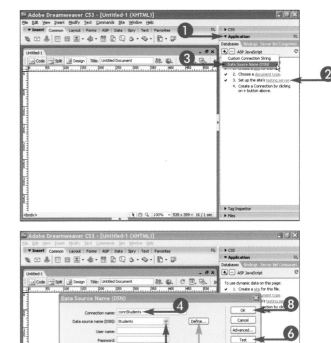

TIP

Can I open dynamic Web pages directly through my browser instead of installing a Testing Server?

No. Web browsers are not capable of understanding server-side programming languages. Instead of displaying a dynamic Web page, the Web browser displays the programming code that comprises the page. Think of the Testing Server as a person who translates the results of this code into HTML, a language that your Web browser understands.

Create a Recordset

You can request retrieval of a recordset — a virtual group of items — from a database. You can then manipulate and display this selection of data on the Web page. A recordset can contain one or more fields, such as the name, address, or phone number fields in a contact database.

Create a Recordset

1 Click **File**.

2 Click **New** to open a new document.

A New Document dialog box appears.

3 Click **Blank Page**.

4 Click **ASP VBScript**.

5 Click **<none>**.

6 Click **Create**.

An untitled page appears.

7 Click the **Bindings** tab.

8 Click ✚.

9 Click **Recordset (Query)**.

The Recordset dialog box appears.

10 Type a name for your recordset.

11 Click ☑.

12 Click a connection.

Your connection is the DSN that you assigned to this site.

***Note:** For more information, see the section, "Configure a Dynamic Web Site."*

TIP

Does it matter if I choose ASP VBScript or ASP JavaScript for new dynamic Web pages?

No, it does not make a difference. Dreamweaver inserts code, either JavaScript or VBScript, to create your dynamic Web pages. The only time that it makes a difference is if you want to make changes to the code that Dreamweaver inserts. If this is the case, then you should choose the scripting language with which you are more familiar. For more information about scripting in ASP pages, visit www.microsoft.com/scripting/ or www.4guysfromrolla.com.

continued

A recordset serves as a temporary mediator between the databases where the information is stored and the dynamic Web page application.

Create a Recordset *(continued)*

⓱ Click ⃝.

⓮ Click the table that you want to use to create a recordset.

⓯ Click **Test** to view the recordset that you have created.

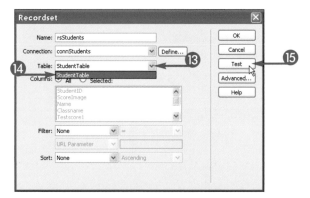

The Test SQL Statement dialog box appears.

⓰ Click **OK** to close the test screen.

Filtering and sorting are optional. If you choose not to set either menu, then your recordset displays everything in the table as it appears in the database.

17 Click **OK** to close the Recordset dialog box.

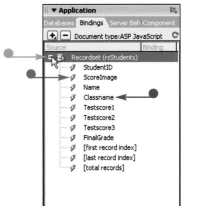

Dreamweaver creates a recordset within your Bindings panel.

● You can click + to expand the column names of your recordset.

● Lightning bolt icons (⚡) represent the table columns in your recordset.

● To modify a recordset, you can double-click its name.

TIP

How do I organize database content on a Web page?

① Create a recordset by following Steps **1** to **16** in this section.

② In the Recordset dialog box, click the **Sort** ☑ and select the field by which you want to sort.

③ Click here and select the condition by which you want to sort, for example, **Ascending** or **Descending**.

④ Click **Test** to preview the sorted results in the Test SQL Statement dialog box.

⑤ Click **OK**.

⑥ Click **OK** to save your sorted recordset.

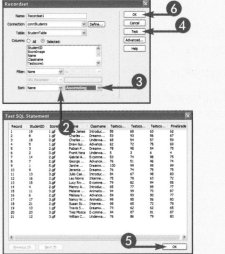

Add a Record

Instead of entering information into your database with desktop software, you can create your own Web page forms that enable you to input content into your database using a Web browser.

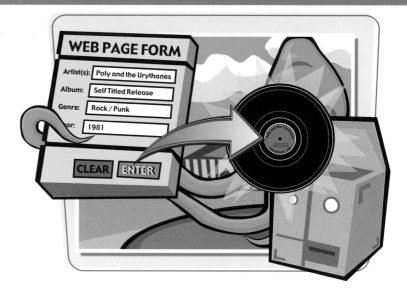

Add a Record

1. Create a recordset containing the tables to which you want to add a record.

Note: For more information, see the section, "Create a Recordset."

2. Click where you want to insert the form.

3. Click **Insert**.

4. Click **Data Objects**.

5. Click **Insert Record**.

6. Click **Record Insertion Form Wizard**.

The Record Insertion Form dialog box appears.

7. Click here and select your connection.

8. Click here and select your table.

9. Click **OK**.

A completed form appears with highlighted fields and assigned server behaviors.

You can open your Web browser and test the page in your Testing Server.

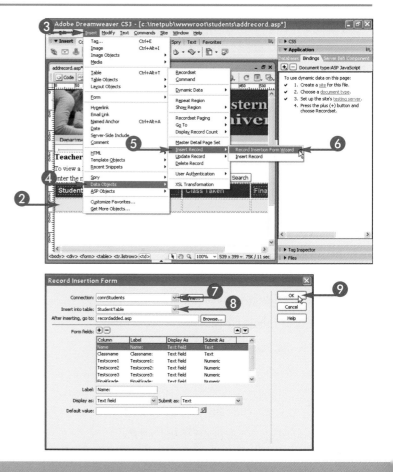

Similar to the Record Insertion Form object, this server object creates a form that allows you to view content from a database in form fields, modify them on the page, and submit your changes back to the database.

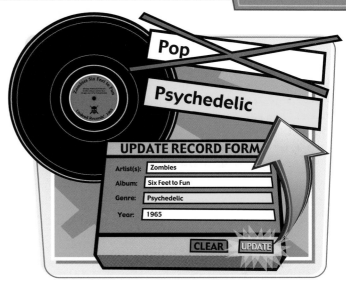

Update a Record

1 Create a recordset containing the tables to which you want to add a record.

Note: For more information, see the section, "Create a Recordset."

2 Click where you want to insert the form.

3 Click **Insert**.

4 Click **Data Objects**.

5 Click **Update Record**.

6 Click **Record Update Form Wizard**.

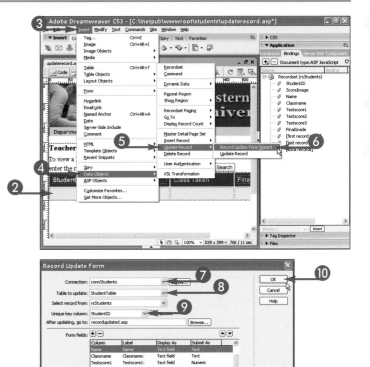

The Record Update Form dialog box appears.

7 Click here and select a connection.

8 Click here and select your table.

9 Click here and select a unique key for the table.

10 Click **OK**.

A highlighted form and Submit button appear.

You can open your Web browser and test the page in your Testing Server.

Add Recordset Paging

You can use the server behavior, Recordset Paging, to display the amount of information that you want on each page. This is useful because most search engines limit their pages to 20 results per page. You can use dynamic links or buttons to navigate to the rest of the content.

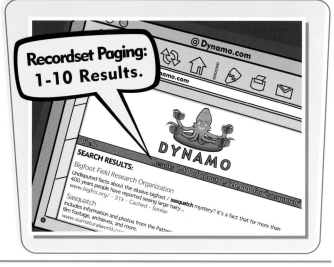

Add Recordset Paging

REPEAT A REGION

1. Select the regions of the page that you want to repeat.

Note: *The region that you select must contain items from your recordset.*

2. Click the **Server Behaviors** tab.

3. Click 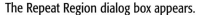.

4. Click **Repeat Region**.

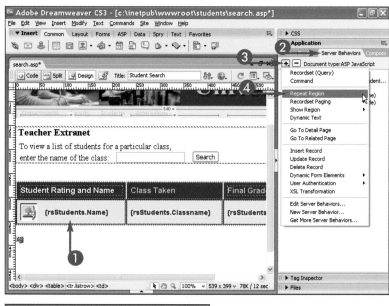

The Repeat Region dialog box appears.

5. Click here and select the recordset that contains the data that you want to repeat.

6. Click **Show** (○ changes to ◉).

7. Type the number of records that you want to appear on a page.

8. Click **OK**.

PAGINATE YOUR DYNAMIC PAGE

A Repeat tab appears around the region that you specified.

⑨ Click the **Server Behaviors** tab.

⑩ Click ⊞.

⑪ Click **Recordset Paging**.

⑫ Click a paging behavior from the menu.

The most commonly used paging behaviors are to move to either the next or the previous record.

⑬ Click 🌐 to preview the page in a Web browser.

A highlighted text link appears on your page.

⑭ Click the new links to browse to the next or previous pages that display the repeating regions with your database content.

The Show Region option enables you to automatically hide navigational links. Click the **Next** button or link, then click **Show Region** from the Server Behaviors panel, and then click **Show If Not Last Record** to control the display of navigation options.

TIP

How can I protect my dynamic forms from hackers?

First, save all of the data-entry screens in an obscurely named area of your Web site. Next, use simple password authentication. IIS allows you to modify the properties of a folder to activate directory security. Finally, install an SSL certificate so that passwords that are sent to unlock this directory cannot be intercepted. To purchase a certificate and to learn more about SSL, visit www.thawte.com and www.verisign.com.

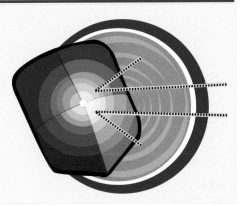

Create a Site Search

You can create a site search to quickly and easily enable Web site visitors to locate records in a database. Creating a site search essentially combines several sections of this chapter. You must create the search form, define the search parameters in a recordset, and then designate where the search results appear with the Repeated Region server behavior.

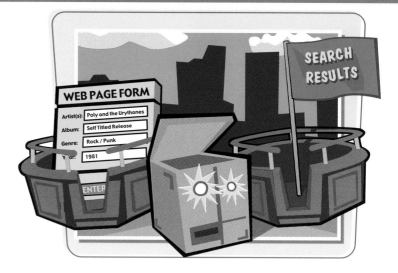

Create a Site Search

① Create a new dynamic page using ASP JavaScript technology.

Note: *For more information, see the section, "Create a Recordset."*

② Create a form with a text field and a Submit button.

The form method should be post, by default.

Note: *To create a form, see Chapter 10.*

③ Type a name for your text field.

④ Click ➕.

⑤ Click **Recordset (Query)** to open the Recordset dialog box.

⑥ Click here and select the connection and table for your site search.

⑦ Click here and select the column in the database that matches the field with which you want to search.

⑧ Click here and select how the filter should behave.

You can select **contains** for flexible searching, or select **=** for exact matches.

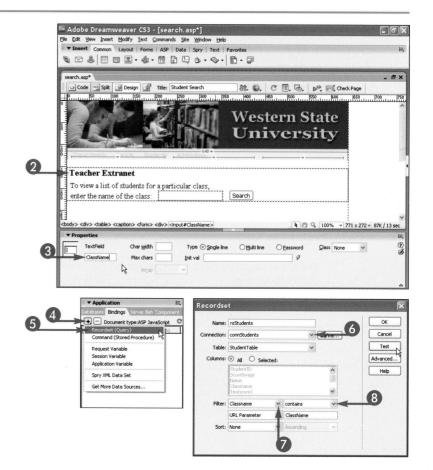

⑨ Click here and select **URL Parameter** as your filter style.

⑩ Type the name of your text field as the filter style variable, using the name of the field that you created in Step 3.

⑪ Click **Test** to open the Please Provide a Test Value dialog box.

⑫ Type a search term that is in the specified area of your database.

⑬ Click **OK**.

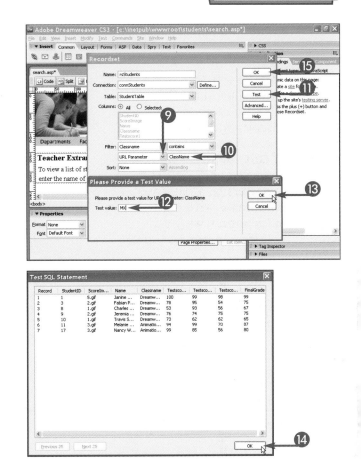

The Test SQL Statement dialog box displays the filtered results.

In this example, the test value was the word MX.

⑭ Click **OK** to close the Test SQL Statement dialog box.

⑮ Click **OK** in the Recordset dialog box to save your filtered recordset.

TIP

How do I create a site search that indexes the Web pages of my site like a search engine?

Dreamweaver does not offer any page-indexing features. However, there are third-party extensions that you can install, as well as manual indexing methods. Visit http://exchange.macromedia.com and search on the term *search*. Atomz Search and Deva Tools are among the best third-party indexing extensions. To create your own index, add a table in your database that contains URLs and keywords about your pages, and then create a site search that looks at those keywords. Your repeated region can then display the URLs to those relevant pages in your database, just as a search engine does.

continued

A Web site user can conduct a site search by formulating a recordset with a dynamic value set. The form allows the user to input what the recordset filters. The user then submits the form, the server behaviors perform the filter script, and the filtered data is returned as a recordset that displays on the Web page.

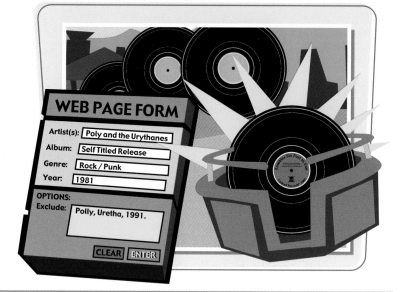

Create a Site Search *(continued)*

⓰ Create a table with the fields from the recordset that you want to display as search results.

Note: *For information on creating a table with fields from a recordset, see the section, "Add a Record."*

⓱ Apply the Repeat Region server behavior to your table.

Note: *For information on repeating a region, see the section, "Add Recordset Paging."*

⓲ Specify the options you want in the Repeat Region dialog box.

⓳ Select your repeat region table.

⓴ Click the **Server Behaviors** tab.

㉑ Click ➕.

㉒ Click **Show Region**.

㉓ Click **Show Region If Recordset Is Not Empty**.

A dialog box appears.

㉔ To confirm your recordset, click here and select it from the drop-down menu.

㉕ Click **OK**.

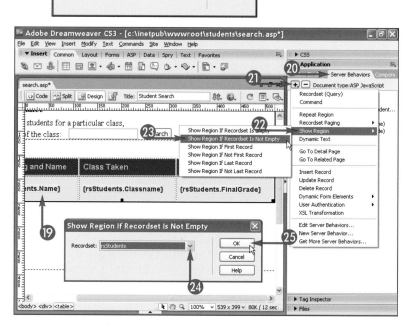

㉖ Preview this page in your Web browser.

㉗ Type a search value in your form.

㉘ Click **Search**.

● The search results appear.

Note: *To apply the Recordset Paging server behavior to help you to navigate through a long list of search results, see the section, "Add Recordset Paging."*

● Remember to apply the appropriate Show Region behaviors to your Next and Previous links. Otherwise, both of these links appear before you perform a search.

TIP

Where can I learn more about creating dynamic Web sites?

Dynamic Web sites are highly complex, and most people who develop sites are highly trained, experienced programmers. This chapter is designed to just introduce you to Dreamweaver's database features. If you want to learn more, visit www.macromedia.com and check out the Developer's section for more information. If you are an Apple user, visit www.mamp.info for more information on dynamic site creation.

Index

Index

Index

Index